D0987098

ILLINOIS PRAIRIE DPL

A65501 488925

TRANSFORMING POWER OF TECHNOLOGY

TRANSFORMING POWER OF TECHNOLOGY

THE STEAM ENGINE

Sara Louise Kras

ILLINOIS PRAIRIE DISTRICT LIBRARY

CHELSEA HOUSE
PUBLISHERS
A Haights Cross Communications Company

Philadelphia

J
621.1
KRA

Frontis: This steam-powered pump for drawing water from mines was designed by Thomas Newcomen in the early 1700s.

CHELSEA HOUSE PUBLISHERS

VP, NEW PRODUCT DEVELOPMENT   Sally Cheney
DIRECTOR OF PRODUCTION   Kim Shinners
CREATIVE MANAGER   Takeshi Takahashi
MANUFACTURING MANAGER   Diann Grasse

Staff for THE STEAM ENGINE

EXECUTIVE EDITOR   Lee Marcott
ASSISTANT EDITOR   Kate Sullivan
PRODUCTION ASSISTANT   Megan Emery
PICTURE RESEARCHER   Amy Dunleavy
SERIES AND COVER DESIGNER   Keith Trego
LAYOUT   21st Century Publishing and Communications Inc.

©2004 by Chelsea House Publishers,
a subsidiary of Haights Cross Communications.
All rights reserved. Printed and bound in the United States of America.

A Haights Cross Communications ◆ Company

http://www.chelseahouse.com

First Printing

1 3 5 7 9 8 6 4 2

Library of Congress Cataloging-in-Publication Data

Kras, Sara Louise.
  Steam engine / by Sara Louise Kras.
    p. cm. — (Transforming power of technology)
Includes index.
Summary: Discusses how the invention of the steam engine transformed
society specifically and how it advanced technology in general.
  ISBN 0-7910-7453-6
  1. Steam-engines—Juvenile literature. [1. Steam engines.] I. Title.
II. Series.
  TJ467.K73 2003
  621.1—dc21
                        2003009483

Before the Steam Engine

AT ISSUE

The word "modern" refers to what is happening today. Prior to the invention of the steam engine, the farming techniques, modes of land and water transportation, and mining methods that were employed were all considered modern. These means seem archaic to us now, but in the late eighteenth and early nineteenth centuries, people could not even conceive of the machines we use and take for granted today. Nor can we imagine the machines and devices that will be created in the future.

Throughout history, improvements were made in how we harnessed first the muscle power of horses and oxen, then windmills, waterwheels, and other devices. None of these improvements, however, even approximated the impact made by the power of steam. Using steam as a source of power was not a novel idea, but harnessing it to drive a machine was a different matter entirely.

To see how the power of steam transformed society, we must first look at life before the advent of the steam engine.

SOURCES OF POWER BEFORE THE STEAM ENGINE

Prior to the steam engine, man relied on his own muscles and those of domesticated animals, wind, and water as sources of power. In Egypt, the muscle power of slaves was used to excavate, haul, and shape huge stones for the Egyptian pyramids. In the sixteenth century, a man walking on the treads of a slanted, round treadmill attached to a millstone would produce the power to grind grain.

One of the many ways that steam has transformed society is by powering trains, like the Grand Canyon Railroad (seen here), which transported increased numbers of passengers and goods at faster speeds than any machines before their invention.

Animals were another source of power. Harnessed oxen, donkeys, and even dogs helped to lay roads as well as to construct temples and palaces. Dogs harnessed to a large wheel were made to run in place to turn a small metal wheel attached to a larger wheel. The small wheel, which would spin quickly due to the force of the larger wheel, was used as a sharpening tool.

Eventually, the energy of running water channeled to turn waterwheels was used to supplement the muscle power of man and beast. A waterwheel has paddles that turn the wheel as water flows across them. The spinning of the waterwheel is converted into energy, or power, by a shaft or pole attached to a millstone or spinning machine.

Waterwheels were used to crush stone, grind grain and

seeds, and pump water up to the surface from deep wells. During the fifteenth century, the waters of streams and ponds powered waterwheels that turned hammers to shape iron.

Wind power was also harnessed in Western Europe. Windmills were usually built on top of a hill to catch the steady flow of the wind. The construction of the sails of a windmill was very important, and its design alone could determine how effectively the windmill responded to wind speed and direction. In order for the windmill to operate, the wind speed had to be at least 15 to 25 miles per hour.

As late as the early nineteenth century, windmills were used to grind corn for cornmeal. Wind power turned large grindstones that crushed the corn kernels underneath. Windmills equipped with large scoops were also used to lift water from marshlands so the land could be farmed.

But waterwheels and windmills were unreliable sources of power. What if there was no wind to turn the windmill? How would the corn be ground? What if the water in a stream froze, making it impossible for the waterwheel to turn? Such questions spurred inventors to continue searching for a consistent and reliable source of power.

MINING BEFORE THE STEAM ENGINE

Mining for minerals took place as early as 27 B.C. in the Roman Empire. By A.D. 1000, coal was the preferred fuel in Europe. It was used for smelting iron, copper zinc, and other ores. The intense heat it produced melted these strong materials or fused them together. The heat from coal was also employed in making glass.

In addition to coal, deep in the ground laid other valuable materials, such as gold, silver, lead, and zinc. These valuable materials were extracted from the earth prior to the invention of the steam engine by digging a hole. The problem was that the deeper the hole, the more water rushed into the area to be mined. This water was removed by hand, which took months

Stagecoaches were the most modern way to travel overland before the invention of the steam engine in the mid-1800s. Passengers had limited room on the stagecoaches, sometimes competing with mailbags for space, and could only bring 25 pounds of luggage. Since stagecoaches were pulled by horses, travel was slow — reaching top speeds of seven or eight miles per hour — and drivers had to stop frequently to refresh their horses.

or even years. Waterwheels were used to pump out the water, but their capabilities were limited. Engineers and inventors tackled the problem and created steam engines to solve it.

LAND TRANSPORTATION BEFORE THE STEAM ENGINE

In the early nineteenth century, before steam engines, traveling was quite a challenge. Roads were mere dirt tracks. When it rained, the dirt became soft, sticky mud that made it nearly impossible to travel. The stagecoach pulled by horses was the most modern mode of land transport. A stagecoach could travel about seven to eight miles per hour. Passengers squeezed into narrow seats and sometimes rode with mailbags on their laps.

They were allowed only 25 pounds of luggage, and many found they had to shed suitcases and boxes before boarding. Horses were changed every 12 to 15 miles at inns built alongside the roads to welcome dusty and weary travelers. The paying guests all ate at the same table and sometimes had to share their rooms and even their beds with strangers.

Sometimes the stage, as it was also called, would travel all night and travelers would sleep in the carriage. Mark Twain recalled one such uncomfortable experience: "First we would all be down in a pile at the forward end of the stage, nearly in a sitting posture, and in a second we would shoot to the other end, and stand on our heads . . . [warding] off ends and corners of mailbags that came lumbering over us." [1]

One could also travel by covered wagon, handcart, or horseback. Oxen, horses, and mules pulled the covered wagons that settlers moving west drove to take their furniture and other belongings to a new home. Handcarts, called the "poor man's covered wagon," however, were not pushed or pulled by domestic animals. They were moved by human power. Horseback was convenient for those traveling light, but gave no protection from weather elements, including rain and snow. Once the steam engine was developed and railroad tracks were laid across the American prairie, traveling was much less difficult.

FARMING PRIOR TO STEAM POWER

Before steam power, farming was mainly done by hand or with the help of oxen or horses. Horses and oxen move at a very slow pace compared to modern-day machines. The farmer walked behind the plow, holding it steady to cut grooves of an even depth in the often hard dirt. He also had to steer the horse at the same time, making plowing a very tough job.

The process of threshing harvested crops separates grain from its chaff. Prior to the steam engine, teams of men did this, but later a machine was developed to do it for them.

Building Up Steam

Many of the components of the steam engine were developed hundreds of years before its creation. In the Alexandrian Empire in A.D. 50, temple doors were automatically closed and opened by utilizing the power of steam.

A fire was lit on the altar, which, unknown to the common observer, was airtight and contained water. Steam pressure forced water out into a bucket. The heavy bucket then pulled down on a rope. The rope was attached to other ropes and pulleys that then opened the temple doors.

The piston and cylinder are key pieces of a working steam engine. Ctesibius, a philosopher from Alexandria, is often credited with the discovery. This tool was used as a fire extinguisher around 200 B.C.

In 1606, Giovanni Battista della Porta of Naples, Italy, wrote down the details of two laboratory experiments that later became the foundation for two different types of steam engine. His first experiment used steam to force water out of a tank and his second experiment used condensing steam to suck water into an upside-down flask.

A French landscaper who heard of these two experiments devised a fountain. He made a round water tank and filled it with water. He then stuck a vertical tube deep into the water so that the top of the tube emerged from the tank. He built a fire under it to heat the water and, once enough steam pressure had built up within the sphere, water spurted high into the air from the tube.

Later, in 1629, an Italian named Giovanni Branca created a machine that drove a wheel by blasting it with steam. Three hundred years later, this discovery was acknowledged as the seed that permitted the creation of the impulse turbine, an engine driven by the pressure of steam. This concept still powers modern-day ships, airplanes, and electrical generators.

All of these experiments paved the way to the invention of the steam engine.

SHIPPING BEFORE STEAM POWER

Before the steam engine, boats sailed by the power of the wind, by men rowing with oars, or by the pull of the water current. Large schooners called merchant ships operated in a manner similar to our trucking systems today. They hauled hay, bricks, lumber, coffee, apples, and many other commodities. Their huge billowy sails filled with wind to push the ships along the coast or across the open ocean. However, transporting people and goods from New York to California by water routes could take many months. The most direct route was to sail south on the Atlantic Ocean, around the southern tip of South America, and then north on the Pacific Ocean. Many stops were required to supply the ship, its crew, and its passengers with fresh water and food.

The clipper ship, a type of schooner, had layers of sails and was touted as the fastest-sailing ship. Clipper ships roamed the globe with their passengers and freight in the nineteenth century. They were also popular with pirates, slave runners, and anyone who needed to make a quick getaway. These ships were swift and steady as long as the wind blew. However, routes sometimes passed through the doldrums, equatorial regions of the ocean filled with eerie calms and light, shifting winds. These doldrums could quickly bring a clipper ship to a standstill and leave it floating in still waters for days.

Warships could carry as many as 12 large cannons. These cannons were packed with gunpowder wrapped in a cloth bag, on top of which a round of ammunition was placed. When the cannon was fired, it recoiled violently back into the ship. Cannons were kept in place with thick ropes, and it took six men to fire each cannon. The sides of some ships were armored with thick iron plates to protect them from the cannonballs of enemy fire.

Smaller boats were also carried aboard some merchant ships and warships. They were maneuvered by sailing or rowing and took men ashore or to explore small water inlets.

Clearly, boats were subjected to limitations prior to the steam engine. Traveling downriver was not a problem as long as the current swiftly took them along. Getting back up the river, however, could be difficult. Men had to row against the current, and if the current or the wind was not in their favor, they were at least temporarily out of luck. Due to these factors, horses or oxen carried most goods upstream. Thus, there was very little upstream traffic on rivers prior to the steam engine.

MANUFACTURING WITHOUT STEAM POWER

The Industrial Revolution began just before the advent of the steam engine. The main fabric used in Europe until the 1600s was wool. Then, cotton imported from India became popular. Wool merchants, who were displeased with this new development, protested the importation of cotton fabric and succeeded in banning it. Businessmen, however, recognized an opportunity to make money and started to import raw cotton. This cotton needed to be made into fabric. Weaving devices were streamlined to allow each weaver to make more fabric. Spinning machines were improved and eventually powered by the waterwheel to increase production. In 1764, James Hargreaves made the Spinning Jenny, a machine that could simultaneously spin eight strands of thread instead of one like the earlier spinning wheels.

Subsequent upgrades to the Spinning Jenny made it difficult to work by hand, so a large waterwheel was used. The waterwheel could power many machines at once. A system of belts and pulleys connected to the waterwheel transferred energy to each machine. Suddenly, weavers had more yarn than they could weave. According to J.D. Storer in his book *A Simple History of the Steam Engine*: "All these improvements in spinning left the weavers struggling to cope with the output of yarn, and in 1785 a new era in weaving began." [2]

In the United States, textile mills were established under the guidance of Samuel Slater, a European immigrant. Prior to the first textile mills, all fabric was made at home. By 1800, a mill might employ up to 100 people. Cotton fabric began to be made at a rapid rate. By 1810, there were over 61 cotton mills with about 31,000 spindles operating in the United States. Because of the moneymaking opportunities near textile mills, families began to move from the countryside into towns. They

The Spinning Jenny was invented by James Hargreaves in 1764. While his invention was revolutionary in itself — spinning cotton eight times faster than prior spinning wheels — waterwheels were eventually introduced to power many machines simultaneously. These new advancements in weaving led to the birth of the textile mill, which played a key role in the Industrial Revolution.

brought their country skills with them and began to bake bread, repair shoes, and plaster the homes of others living and working in the vicinity.

These country families had many children, who were soon put to work in the textile mills. Their small fingers were the right size to work with yarn. Children were paid less than adults, but even so, their parents wanted them to work to make extra money for the household. Ten-year-old children worked as long as 11 hours a day in the textile mills. Children continued to work these long hours even after steam engines replaced the waterwheels. It wasn't until 1904, when the National Child Labor Committee was formed, that these child labor abuses ended.

Shipbuilding and furniture-making were other industries of the eighteenth century. Most of this work was done by hand. Shipping played a large role in bringing desirable goods from faraway foreign lands, such as the exotic woods that were crafted into beautiful furniture for wealthy families.

The Industrial Age sharply affected the ways families lived. Before the proliferation of textile mills, everything was done in the home. Women and children stayed home and spun wool, made clothing, and farmed crops. As mills increasingly became the sites for production, people began working outside the home. These workers earned money to buy things that used to be made in the home. The establishment of the textile mills was only the beginning of this change in lifestyle. Once the steam engine became a practical and useful machine, factories and assembly lines were employed to use the power it supplied for doing other types of jobs and creating other products.

Although it took many years for a practical steam engine to be developed, the idea of using steam as a source of power was not new. An inventor living in the Alexandrian Empire in A.D. 60 was one of the first to realize its potential. During this time, an extensive library in Alexandria, Egypt, contained much of the knowledge of the world. Scholars and students came from all over the world to study its texts. One of the many scholars who studied there experimented with the power of steam. Eventually, the Alexandrian library was destroyed and a great portion of its information was lost forever.

2 Early Inventors of the Steam Engine

Although the power of steam had been observed long before, there was no practical way to employ steam to replace muscle, wind, or water. In the seventeenth century, visionary men began to experiment with ways to capture steam power. These inventors, dissatisfied with the current power sources, labored to discover other means to accomplish tasks. By doing so, they brought the world into a new era, an era in which mechanical devices eased the hardships of man.

Robert H. Thurston, professor of mechanical engineering and author of a history of the steam engine, wrote, "Great inventions are never, and great discoveries are seldom, the work of any one mind. . . . It is not a creation but a *growth*—as truly so as that of the trees in the forest."[3] This chapter discusses the many men who contributed to the development of the steam engine.

HERO OF ALEXANDRIA

The first inventor of the steam engine, a man named Hero, lived around A.D. 60 in the Alexandrian Empire. In his notes, Hero describes in detail what is thought to be the first working steam engine, which he called an "aeolipile." His design consisted of a sealed kettle of water that was placed over a fire. Attached to the kettle on both sides were two thin pipes. These led up to a hollow metal ball. The ball had two bent tubes, which allowed steam to escape. As the water boiled, steam rose into the pipes and then into the hollow sphere, making it rotate at a rapid speed. The aeolipile, rather than being considered useful, was seen as an interesting toy.

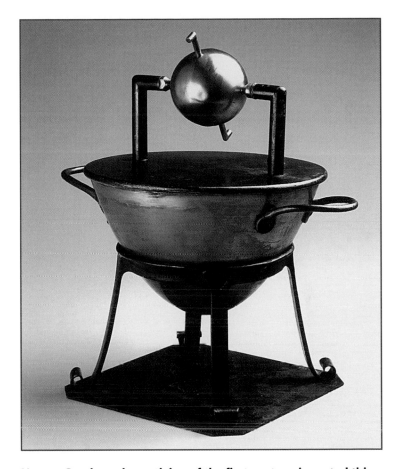

Hero, a Greek mathematician of the first century, invented this early steam engine. Called an aeolipile, it was a hollow ball into which steam from the sealed cauldron of boiling water rose. The short pipes extending from the ball were bent at a right angle and emitted jets of the highly pressurized steam, causing the ball to rotate.

Hero was very interested in "how 'vapours of water' could be harnessed to create contrived effects. Jets of steam could make a horn blow or a bird sing or a hollow ball whirl around, and in religious rituals an extra element of mystery could be achieved." [4]

OTTO VON GUERICKE

Otto von Guericke, a German physicist, lived from 1602 to 1686. He was fascinated by the possibility of harnessing the force of atmospheric pressure. Through his experiments, von Guericke proved that without air pressure a ringing bell has no sound and animals cannot live.

In 1654, von Guericke invented the first air pump, which he used in his famous experiment of the Magdeburg hemispheres. These half-spheres of metal were greased along the edges and then fitted together to make a round ball. All the air inside the ball was pumped out to create a vacuum. Von Guericke, to prove that the vacuum would seal the two half-spheres together, tied eight horses to each one. The 16 horses pulled and pulled, but the two halves would not separate. Once von Guericke opened the air tap at the top of the ball, however, the pressure was released and the halves fell apart.

To further prove the power of atmospheric pressure, von Guericke had 20 men raise a large piston in a cylinder. He then emptied air out of the cylinder. After a valve in the cylinder was opened, air rushed in and pulled down the piston despite the best efforts of the 20 men. These two experiments proved that atmospheric pressure was a source of energy.

DENIS PAPIN

Denis Papin, a French inventor who lived from 1647 to 1714, was fascinated by the power of steam. Papin made many inventions while he experimented with steam. One of them was the pressure cooker, an airtight container that cooked food quickly by pressure under steam. Another was a steam engine. He used his engine to lift water from one canal to another and to pump water from a canal into a tank that supplied water fountains on the estate of his benefactor.

In 1690, Papin developed a piston-and-cylinder engine that was driven by steam pressure. He refined the engine to include

The Many Uses of Steam

Many of the machines developed to use steam power aren't very well known. A French inventor, Henri Giffard, built a steam-powered airship in 1852. Its 11-foot, three-bladed propeller moved the ship through the air at five miles per hour. He steered the large airship with a sail-type rudder. The 17-mile flight was the first controlled flight of a working airship.

Later, in 1858, Giffard invented the steam injector, which was used throughout the world in locomotive engines.

The construction industry also employed the steam engine to power crane lifts, which lifted heavy items at construction sites and loaded and unloaded ships; steam-powered rollers used to flatten dirt for roads; and huge steam shovels that scooped dirt from the ground for construction or mining purposes.

Early elevators were powered by steam, as were drawbridges. Clouds of steam would float over the river as the engines raised the massive bridges up to clear the way for passing steam freighters.

Even lawn mowers became powered by steam. Prior to this, small lawn mowers were pushed by hand. Larger lawn mowers had to be pushed by two people or pulled by horses. In 1893, James Sumner of Lancashire, England, developed the first steam-powered lawn mower by basically taking a horse-drawn mower and placing a steam engine on top of it. The steam engine was fueled by oil rather than coal. The mower was so expensive that only the wealthy could afford it, usually to mow huge lawns or stadiums. The main complaint about the steam-powered mower was that it took as long to heat up the steam engine as it did to mow the lawn!

safety valves that released some of the steam when the pressure built up to an explosive level.

After Papin made his many inventions using steam, he wrote about his discoveries in *The New Art of Pumping Water by Using Steam,* published in 1707.

Papin was a firm believer in the potential of steam power. He asserted that steam power was much better than water power. He said "to those—and they were the majority—who suggested that 'the power of rivers' would be more effective, . . . 'there are

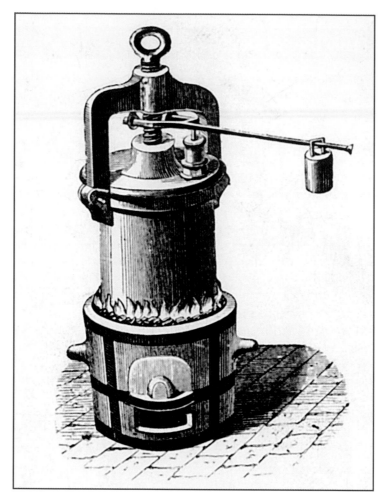

This pressure cooker was invented by Denis Papin, a French physicist, in the 1680s. The sealed pot on a furnace base cooked foods quickly with pressurized steam. Papin was captivated by the power of steam and developed many machines to harness its power.

many cases where rivers are completely lacking or are so distant that the maintenance of a machine would cost almost as much as if water was raised by human power.'" [5]

Papin worked on other inventions besides the steam engine,

such as the structure of the submarine and a grenade launcher. He then moved to London, where he was unknown, and died a few years later in poverty.

Until this time, the pursuit of a workable steam engine was more of a diversion than a necessity. However, mining started to become very important in Europe, and pumping water out of deep mines was still an unsolved and perplexing problem.

THOMAS SAVERY

The first man to build and sell a workable steam engine was Thomas Savery. He was born in 1650 and died in 1715. When he was 48 years old, this English inventor patented his developments on the steam engine. The patent granted him the right to be the only person to sell, produce, or profit from his invention of an "'engine' for raising water. . . 'by the impellent force of fire.'" [6] The patent stayed in effect until 1733.

Savery's goal was to create a reliable machine to pump water out of mines. He developed a model of his machine and presented it to the Royal Society in 1699. The presentation was considered a success. Later, in 1702, his book explaining his invention, *The Miner's Friend, or an Engine to Raise Water by Fire Described,* was published.

Savery "claimed that his pumping engine could replace 10 or 12 horses because it could raise 'as much water as two Horses working together at one time . . . and for which there must be constantly kept ten or twelve horses.'" [7]

The engine had no moving parts except for hand-operated valves that were opened and closed when they were turned. The first steam engine used the power of atmospheric pressure, which had been discovered by von Guericke 40 years earlier.

This machine had several drawbacks. It could only pump water from 50 feet below. Also, too many switches and checks were required to keep the machine running continuously. There were cold and hot water valves that had to be switched every four minutes, the water level in the main boiler had to be checked constantly and refilled when necessary, and in addition, the fire had to be stoked continually to keep the water hot.

The biggest problem Savery faced was creating a boiler that could withstand the intense heat. His boilers, which were quite small, held about five to six gallons of water. When Savery tried to increase the pressure and temperature of the steam, the solder keeping the metal boiler together would soften and melt. Joints were then used to fasten the metal plates together with a hard solder. Even then, the boiler walls still needed to be strengthened. Many years later, after Savery died, metal rivets were used to hold steam boilers together.

Savery was the first man to control the power of steam. He was convinced that steam would be used for power in the future. He pictured "occasioning Motion to all sorts of Mill Work . . . and for the working of all sorts of Mills where they have not the Benefit of Water nor constant Windes." [8]

Savery was the first to make a working steam engine, however impractical it was to use. Not until a man named Thomas Newcomen began his experiments would the steam engine be given a practical design.

THOMAS NEWCOMEN

Thomas Newcomen was born in 1663 in Dartmouth, England. When he grew up, he apprenticed as a hardware dealer and blacksmith. He married in 1705 and his home became a meeting place for dedicated Baptists. During this time, Newcomen also became an active preacher.

When traveling on business, Newcomen often visited tin mines. In conversations with the miners, he must have discovered that there was a need for a machine to remove water from the deep mines. The miners did not have access to large streams that could power waterwheels and draft animals were not strong enough to pull the water up from such great depths.

Little is known about Newcomen's early experiments because he did not belong to a circle of inventors, nor did he

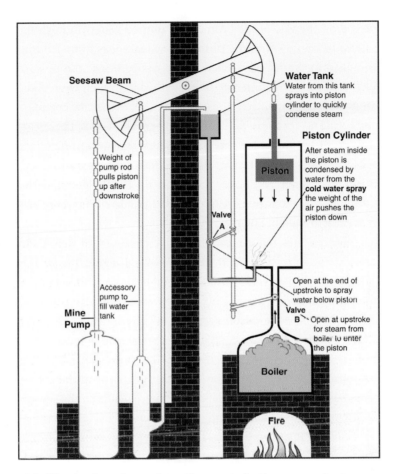

Seesaw Beam

Water Tank
Water from this tank
sprays into piston
cylinder to quickly
condense steam

Weight of
pump rod
pulls piston
up after
downstroke

Piston Cylinder
After steam inside
the piston is
condensed by
water from the
cold water spray
the weight of the
air pushes the
piston down

Piston

Valve
A

Accessory
pump to
fill water
tank

Open at the end of
upstroke to spray
water below piston

**Mine
Pump**

Valve
B   Open at upstroke
for steam from
boiler to enter
the piston

Boiler

Fire

**This illustration shows how the parts in Newcomen's steam
engine work together to draw water from mines. Newcomen's
steam engine was the first machine developed to utilize steam
power to complete tasks.**

have a wealthy patron to support his experiments. There is,
however, documentation of one of his earlier machines. It was
a vertically oriented cylinder fitted with a sliding piston. The
piston was connected to a crossbeam—called a seesaw beam—
that moved up and down. The piston was on one side of the
beam and the pump was on the other side of the beam. On each
end of the beam, weights were placed. Heavier weights were

placed on the side of the beam that pumped water. To push the seesaw beam down on the piston side, steam was funneled into the piston cylinder. This filled in the cavity below the upward piston. Then, a lead jacket filled with cold water cooled the steam, which condensed it. The cooling of the steam created a vacuum and lowered the piston side of the seesaw beam by the force of atmospheric pressure. When the pump side of the seesaw beam was pushed up, the underground pump that was filled with water rose. The water was then forced out above ground. Then the whole cycle repeated again to pump more and more water from below the ground.

Newcomen's biggest problem was cooling the hot steam quickly enough. By accident, he discovered a solution to this problem. One day while he was experimenting with the engine, the lead jacket developed a hole. Cold water rushed out of the lead jacket. The cold water speeded up the condensation of the steam within the cylinder and as a result the piston crash down, breaking the chain to which it was attached. This accident prompted Newcomen to come up with the idea to fit the engine with a cold-water spray, which contributed greatly to the success of later models of the Newcomen steam engine.

This piston-and-cylinder engine was the first one developed to have a practical purpose using steam power to complete tasks. It also became the model for all future steam engine developments.

Newcomen was not associated with Savery, and it is uncanny that he was perfecting the very engine that Savery had patented. A Swedish engineer who met Newcomen wrote that "Thomas Newcomen, without any knowledge whatever of the speculations of Captain Savery, had at the same time made up his mind . . . to invent a fire machine for drawing water from the mines." [9]

Newcomen pursued a slightly different method than Savery did for creating enough steam for his engine. Rather than having small boilers, he used larger boilers that contained up to 13 gallons of water.

Newcomen spent about 12 years perfecting his steam engine, and then he made a full-scale model. He installed it in 1710 at a tin mine, but had little success pumping out the water. The technology available to him made the cylinders very difficult to bore precisely enough to allow the piston to move smoothly up and down. This problem continued for many years.

Later, in 1712, after making adjustments to his engine, he installed another one at a coal mine in Staffordshire. The entire engine was about 50 feet tall. One end of the enormous seesaw beam was hooked up to the piston, which was driven up and down within the cylinder by hot steam and atmospheric pressure. The other end of the beam had long pumping rods extending deep into the earth to pump out the water. Newcomen's engine was a fantastic advancement in the use of steam.

The cost of maintaining these engines was enormous because a huge amount of coal was needed to keep them running. These steam engines were most commonly used to pump water out of coal mines. This worked out well because the coal in the mines provided the engine with the fuel it needed to operate.

Because of Savery's patent, Newcomen was unable to sell his machine without paying high royalties to Savery and his successors. Despite this obstacle, Newcomen built over 100 engines in his lifetime. They were being used in many countries, including Great Britain, Germany, Sweden, and France. However, Newcomen never benefited financially from his engine; he died almost unknown in 1729. Newcomen's advancements, unlike his name, lived on for many years. His invention was so effective that it remained unchanged for almost 50 years. With Newcomen's steam engine, the Industrial Revolution had begun. But no one pushed it along faster than James Watt.

3 The Contributions of James Watt

Even though a workable steam engine had been devised by Newcomen, its purpose and function were limited to pumping water. In addition, there was little public interest in taking the development any further—that is, until factories started springing up all over Great Britain, continental Europe, and the United States. Demand for mechanical power was at an all-time high and inventors worked hard to improve existing machines.

In 1764, James Hargreaves improved upon the existing spinning wheel. His invention, called the Spinning Jenny, spun yarn eight times faster than the old spinning wheel. Later, the inventor Richard Arkwright and two friends modified the Spinning Jenny. Their improvements, however, made it almost impossible to turn the wheel by hand. Instead, a waterwheel had to power it.

Samuel Crompton combined the ideas of Hargreaves and Arkwright and invented a machine called the Mule. It had 48 spindles running at the same time. These slender rods would twist, wind, and hold the thread on the spinning machine. The thread produced by the Mule was fine and strong.

All of these inventions left weavers overwhelmed with the huge amounts of yarn that needed to be woven into fabric. Powered looms began to be invented and mills sprang up to support these large machines. Both spinning machines and looms had to be powered, many of them by huge waterwheels, but unfortunately there were not enough water sources. The need for a consistent working engine grew. James Watt would fill this need by further developing the capabilities of the steam engine.

James Watt, a Scotsman asked in 1763 to repair a Newcomen steam engine, did much more than fix it. Over a period of 10 years, he improved its efficiency and power by attaching a condenser and air pump to the cylinder and piston, among other innovations.

HOW IT BEGAN

James Watt was born into an educated family in Scotland in 1736. When he was 27 years old, he was asked by a professor at Glasgow University to repair a Newcomen-type engine.

While working on the engine, Watt realized that it wasted a huge quantity of heat as it ran. He found that the boiler was not creating enough steam and that more water was needed to condense the steam. Also, the materials used to cast the cylinder did not efficiently hold in the heat. Because of this, a lot of the steam's heat was wasted on each stroke of the piston.

Watt mulled over the problems with the Newcomen engine and thought of a possible solution one day while out walking. He built a model to see if attaching a condenser and

ILLINOIS PRAIRIE DISTRICT LIBRARY

an air pump to the cylinder and sliding piston of Newcomen's engine would work.

"Watt avoided cooling his cylinder by condensing the steam in [a] separate condenser, which was connected to the cylinder. This condenser was kept cool with cold water while the cylinder remained hot." [10] The air pump sucked air out of the condenser, creating a vacuum and forcing steam from the hot cylinder to be sucked into the condenser. The hot air immediately condensed and moved the piston. It took Watt 10 years to create a workable engine using his new discovery.

During that time, he befriended John Roebuck of Birmingham, England. Roebuck had coal mines that were continually being flooded. The mines needed a much stronger pumping machine than what was available. In 1768, Roebuck agreed to pay off Watt's debts, finance his inventions, and pay to have his engine patented in exchange for partial financial ownership—called shares—of Watt's inventions. Watt obtained the patent "for a method of lessening the consumption of steam and fuel in fire-engines" [11] in 1769.

Watt immediately built a small building near Birmingham to house his experimental engine. During this time, he tried several different methods for efficiently cooling and heating the piston.

However, Watt was not a focused man. He enjoyed making scientific gadgets and was very skilled at repairing musical instruments. He was also known to make pottery and trained to be a land surveyor. Because of his many skills, he often went from one project to another. In his spare time, he experimented with various inventions that had nothing to do with steam power.

WATT'S BUSINESS PARTNER, MATTHEW BOULTON

Meanwhile, Roebuck ran into financial troubles and filed for bankruptcy. Another businessman, Matthew Boulton, had been watching Watt with interest for several years. He owned

Conflict Over Watt's Patent

After Watt patented his steam engine in 1769, anyone attempting to make a steam engine or using one of his steam engines had to pay a set fee called a royalty to Boulton and Watt.

It was very difficult to prevent others from copying and using Watt's steam engine. Once a person was discovered violating the patent, it was equally difficult to collect the dues owed to Boulton and Watt. Legal fees to fight against violations of their patent were quite expensive. In 1799, they calculated that they had spent at least £10,000 (equal to $15,000) on legal fees. Also, of £300,000 owed to them for violations, they had received only £100,000. After chasing down debtors for many years, they managed to recover some of that money.

Watt did not even try to patent some of his other inventions, such as the governor and the steam engine indicator; all the difficulties he encountered with people violating his steam engine patent made him unwilling to get involved in any more drawn-out legal battles.

Because Watt's patent was in effect for 32 years, it was very difficult for new inventors to expand on his ideas. One critic of Watt and his patent was Joseph Bramah, an engineer. He contended that "Watt had taken out his patent rights not for what he had invented, but for what he might invent in the future."*

Criticism of his patent led Watt to write a statement entitled "Thoughts upon Patents, or exclusive Privileges for new Inventions." In it, he argued, "The 'man of ingenuity' had to 'devote the whole powers of his mind to one object . . . and had to persevere in spite of the many fruitless experiments he makes.'"**

Watt did not believe that his patent had inhibited further discoveries or inventions related to the steam engine. Others disagreed, however, because Watt would not expand his patent "for a method of lessening the consumption of steam and fuel in fire-engines" to include using high-pressure steam. He was opposed to the idea, and his opposition stopped all further progress. Little did Watt know that high-pressure steam engines would be the driving force in steam locomotive transportation.

* Asa Briggs, *The Power of Steam*. Chicago: The University of Chicago Press, 1982, p. 59.
** Ibid.

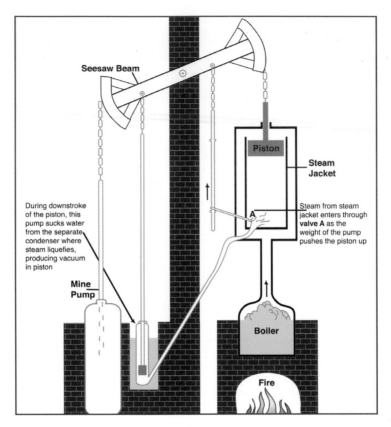

During downstroke of the piston, this pump sucks water from the separate condenser where steam liquefies, producing vacuum in piston

Seesaw Beam

Piston

Steam Jacket

Steam from steam jacket enters through **valve A** as the weight of the pump pushes the piston up

Mine Pump

Boiler

Fire

This illustration of Watt's basic steam engine includes a steam jacket, which he added to Newcomen's model to condense the steam more quickly, and an air pump, which sucks air out of the condenser, creating a vacuum that forces steam from the hot cylinder into the condenser. The hot air immediately condenses and moves the piston.

Boulton's Soho Manufactory, which made small metal objects such as buttons, chains, and steel watches. His water power source, the Hockley Brook, did not provide enough energy for his manufactory. When he heard of Roebuck's financial problems, he quickly bought Roebuck's shares in Watt's inventions, and in 1773 Boulton and Watt officially became business partners.

By 1776, Watt had created his first engines and drawn up designs for new ones. His personal life was also starting to take off. Watt's first wife had died many years earlier and now, at the age of 40, he was preparing to wed again. However, his prospective father-in-law was not very impressed with Watt or his inventions. He insisted on seeing a legal contract between Watt and Boulton in order to define their working relationship. The partners had never created such a document, and Watt pleaded with Boulton in a letter: "I find that the old gentleman wishes to see the contract of Partnership between you and I. . . . I must beg the favour of you to get a legal contract written and signed by yourself, sent by return of post or as soon as may be."[12]

Boulton provided a summary of the fictitious contract, and the bride's father allowed her to marry Watt.

STEAM ENGINE ADVANCES

Watt's machines used a third of the amount of coal that the Newcomen engines used. They became known as coal savers and orders for the machines poured in.

Inventors inspired by the new machine raced to turn the up-and-down motion of the pistons into a circular motion. Patents were issued for cranks and other devices to attach to the steam engine. During this time, Watt constructed a device called a sun and planet gear, two toothed wheels connected to a crankshaft that transferred the piston's up-and-down motion into a quick, circular motion. But because of the jerky motion of the atmospheric machine, these inventions seemed impractical and did not catch on right away. Watt tackled this problem next.

Until 1780, all steam engines were considered to be atmospheric machines because the condensed steam created a vacuum. The vacuum made atmospheric pressure push the piston down. Watt was not happy with this design because the motion was too jerky. He worked to find a way for the piston to be both pushed up and pushed down by steam. This is called a double-acting engine. "He reali[z]ed that he could thus double the performance or power in the same time with a cylinder the same size."[13] He patented this engine in 1782.

Further experiments lead to the discovery of parallel motion. Instead of using a chain to connect the piston to the beam, Watt created a parallel motion device. It allowed the piston to perform in a perfectly straight up-and-down motion even though the beam moved in an arc motion. The parallel motion invention made it possible to transfer power to the upward stroke of the beam as well as the downward stroke. Prior to the parallel motion device, only the downward stroke of the beam had power.

While Watt was working on the sun and planet gear, he began exploring how to define the strength of each engine. The machine's power was compared to how much horses could generate by pulling, so the figure was stated as the number of horses it could replace and the term "horsepower" was born. For example, prior to the steam engine there were machines called roundabouts, which were wheel frames laid on the ground to which two horses were harnessed. The horses walked around and around, turning the wheel, which then turned a millstone that crushed grain. An engine that could replace these two horses with the same amount of power was a two-horsepower engine. Watt was the first to quantify the power of an engine in units of horsepower, such as 14-horse engines or 20-horse engines. This term is still used today to quantify engine strength.

So far, all steam engine pistons moved up and down— vertically. Converting this motion into a circle or situating the cylinder horizontally was next to impossible. But inventors were starting to explore the idea of road travel, and carriages would require a horizontal piston whose work could be converted into a circular motion to drive the wheels. To address this need, Watt created the first horizontal-motion steam engine, with a piston that went from left to right.

By 1784, Watt was supplying engines that moved wheels. These rotating engines became very popular. To ensure that the engines ran smoothly, Boulton and Watt wrote 24 instructions for engine care. "The first direction was 'everything to be kept as clean as possible,' and instruction number 19 was to clean the boiler 'at least once a month, but if the water be muddy . . . more frequently, as it will otherwise not only be liable to destruction by burning, but will likewise require more coals.'" [14]

Watt later reflected on his inventions and wrote in 1808, "Though I am not over anxious after fame, yet I am more proud of the parallel motion than of any other mechanical invention I have ever made." [15]

To measure the performance of an engine, Watt created a device called the steam engine indicator in 1790. Its purpose was to measure the different pressures inside the engine cylinder. "The device was so useful that it was described as the 'engineer's stethoscope.'" [16]

Another important invention of Watt's was a device called a governor, which regulated the speed of an engine. He created it by altering a mechanism previously used in wind-driven flour mills. Use of a regulator was also very important when spinning wool because the number of revolutions per minute had to stay at a constant pace. Watt's governor consisted of a pair of arms attached at a joint to a vertical rod. At the bottom of each arm was a metal ball. As the governor rotated, the balls flew out to the sides of the vertical rod. The top of the vertical rod was connected to a horizontal pole jointed into another vertical rod. The bottom of this second vertical rod was connected to a valve that opened and closed depending on the speed of the spinning balls. If the engine was running fast, the balls flew farther away from their vertical rod and caused the valve connected to the second vertical rod to close by a certain amount. Conversely, if the speed decreased too much, the balls

This statue commemorates the contributions of businessman Matthew Boulton, inventor James Watt, and Watt's assistant (and inventor in his own right) William Murdock to the steam engine. The work of these three Birmingham men greatly improved the steam engine, making it possible to measure pressure and regulate the speed of the engine.

revolved closer to the vertical rod, causing the valve to open and increase the supply of steam.

By the end of the nineteenth century, Boulton and Watt had sold about 500 engines. Steam engines were powering metalworking, printing, and papermaking. Pulp used to make paper was passed through steam-filled cylinders to dry it. Steam-powered cutting and folding machines made it into sheets of paper or envelopes. Steam turned grindstones to sharpen needles for sewing and millstones to make cocoa flakes. Every part of industry was affected by the power of steam. The demand for goods and for faster transporting of raw materials increased at an alarming rate. Still, when Watt was 64 years old, he and Boulton decided to retire and leave the inventions to their sons. New inventors with new ideas would take James Watt's steam engine to even greater heights.

4

Steamboats and Ocean Steamers

Prior to the development of steam-powered boats, it was impossible to move goods upstream. Large sailing ships crossing the Atlantic Ocean that hit the doldrums were stalled and had to wait for wind. This cost time, money, and sometimes lives.

On land, the steam engine was being used as a stationary beam engine to pump water from mines deep underground. It was also powering machinery in factories and driving carriages.

In the nineteenth century, shipping routes were the superhighways of today and sailing ships were the cargo trucks. Speed and reliability in moving goods from one place to another were of prime importance.

Early inventors such as John Fitch, Patrick Miller, and Robert Fulton transferred steam power from land to water. Passenger and cargo steamboats along the Mississippi River were based on their models. Later, huge trans-Atlantic steam liners using the same technology were constructed and forever changed travel.

JOHN FITCH AND PATRICK MILLER

John Fitch, a creative mechanic from Connecticut, engineered a boat that used steam to drive its paddles in 1787. Six paddles on the sides of the boat's hull were moved by a single-cylinder steam engine. Fitch made several runs on the Delaware River with this boat, which went about three miles per hour. A few years later, he built another steamboat, but this time placed the

In 1787, John Fitch's first steamboat was outfitted with six paddles on each side of its hull. The paddles were powered by a single cylinder steam engine, moving the boat along at a speed of three miles per hour. The addition of steam power to watercraft made it possible to move goods upstream, expediting overseas transport.

paddles at the back of the boat. Christened the *Experiment*, it was used to ferry paying customers. Unfortunately, Fitch's business sense was not as sharp as his ingenuity, and he died a financial failure.

Later, in 1801, Edinburgh banker Patrick Miller made several boats propelled by paddle wheels. At that time, men or horses were used to turn the paddle wheels. One of the paddlers, James Taylor, felt the system was archaic and needed the help of the steam engine. He introduced Miller to William Symington, who was a steam engineer. Symington eagerly took on the project and made a small working model that included a steam engine with two huge cylinders and a boiler in the middle of the boat. Two large paddle wheels were placed in the front and the back of the boat. The model worked, so a full-size boat was made. However, neither Fitch nor Symington and Miller had commercial success with their steamboats. It wasn't until Robert Fulton came along that steamboats started to get the public's attention.

ROBERT FULTON

Robert Fulton is thought to have been the inventor of the steamboat. After living in England and France for many years and associating with Boulton and Watt, the American returned to the United States and in 1807 built a steamboat called the *Clermont*. The boat had a deep, V-shaped hull with two large paddle wheels called side-wheels attached to its sides. This steamboat paddled smoothly on the deep Hudson River during its first successful trip from New York City upriver to Albany, New York.

When the boat was tried in the shallow Mississippi River, its hull dragged along the bottom and its side-wheel paddles got tangled in uprooted trees in the water. The boat was then redesigned with a flattened bottom and only one paddle wheel at the back, or stern, of the boat. This type of boat was called a stern-wheeler.

The steam engine was attached to a pumping piston, which was attached to the paddle wheel via an arm. This made the wheel turn either forward or backward, depending on the direction in which the captain wanted the boat to go. Rudders behind and in front of the paddle wheel were used to steer to the left or right. The captain steered the boat from the pilot-house, which was on the highest level of the boat.

During this time, pioneers were settling the Minnesota Territory. The new steamboats played a major role in trans-porting the settlers and their belongings. A half-million people traveled from the mouth of the Mississippi in New Orleans, Louisiana, to St. Paul, Minnesota. Crowded stern-wheelers

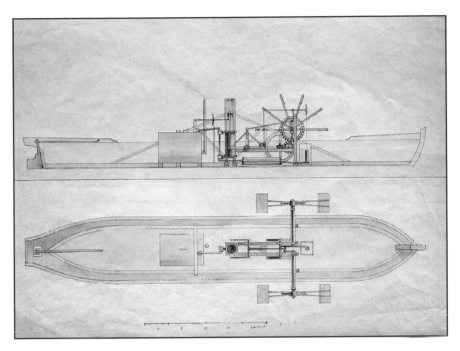

This steamboat diagram was prepared by Robert Fulton, an American who built the steam-driven *Clermont* in 1807. The *Clermont* had two large paddle wheels positioned on each side of the boat. These two wheels were connected by arms to a pumping piston, which was attached to the steam engine. Power from the steam engine would rotate the wheels, forcing the boat into motion.

traveled the river every day. They also carried supplies such as gunpowder, tools, and cloth to isolated areas upstream. On the return trip, they brought animal furs and handmade items. Not all steamboats were cargo ships, however. Showboats brought dancing and music and traveling theater companies. Their whistle blasts were loud and unique to attract the attention of the people onshore.

Mark Twain, the famous American author who grew up and wrote about life on the Mississippi River, described the Mississippi steamboats: "The boat *is* rather a handsome sight. . . . She has two tall, fancy-topped chimneys . . . a fanciful pilothouse, all glass and 'gingerbread' . . . the furnace doors are open and the fires glaring bravely; the upper decks are black with passengers . . . great volumes of the blackest smoke are rolling and tumbling out of the chimneys." [17]

Steamboats had about a five-year life expectancy. The boat usually sank when the boilers eventually overheated and blew up, causing a fire. Several steamboat hulls lay under the waters of the Mississippi River, making it difficult for steamboat captains to maneuver through the water.

Captains were proud of their steamboats and liked to boast about their speed, each claiming that his steamboat was the fastest on the Mississippi. To prove this, they held steamboat races. The most famous race took place in 1870 between the *Natchez* and the *Robert E. Lee*. Sailing between New Orleans and St. Louis, the captains ran their boilers so hot that they almost burst. The men below shoveling coal sweated and groaned as they fed the blazing furnaces. Red flames and sparks flew from the boats' jagged stovepipe chimneys. Spectators along the shore cheered and yelled as the boats sailed by. After three days, eighteen hours, and fourteen minutes, the *Robert E. Lee* crossed the finish line to be crowned the Fastest Boat on the Mississippi.

THE *SAVANNAH*

The SS *Savannah* was the first steam-powered vessel to cross the Atlantic Ocean several times. The ship's captain, Moses Rogers, commissioned Stephen Vail to build the ship's engine. Rogers was convinced that the future of shipping lay in steamers. An associate of Robert Fulton, Rogers was very familiar with how steamboat engines functioned.

The *Savannah* was designed as a sailing ship, but was also equipped with a steam engine and paddle wheels. When the wind died down, the steam engine would power the ship. The doldrums of the Atlantic Ocean would pose no problem for this new and revolutionary ship.

To appeal to the traveling public, the *Savannah*'s luxurious rooms were fitted with mahogany paneling, full-length mirrors, and brass ornaments. Despite these accommodations, the *Savannah* was nicknamed the "Steam Coffin" and shunned by passengers, shipping companies, and crews fearful of fire from the sparks spitting from its chimney.

The *Savannah*'s historic trip across the Atlantic began on May 22, 1819. Departing from Savannah, Georgia, it sailed for England, with plans to stop in Sweden, Russia, Norway, and Denmark before heading back to the United States.

As the *Savannah* approached the coast of Ireland, a signal-station attendant onshore who saw the billows of black smoke assumed the ship was on fire and dispatched a speedy boat to sail out and rescue the burning ship. After chasing the *Savannah* for four or five hours, the rescuing boat's captain realized that the ship was not on fire, but rather was being powered by its own steam. The "rescue" story soon became a running joke in many Irish and English newspapers.

The crew of the *Savannah* was welcomed by royalty in every country it visited. Parties were thrown aboard the steamer to celebrate the modern miracle.

Even though the *Savannah* received worldwide praise, it was still a financial failure. The public felt it was unsafe to travel the ocean on a fire-spitting steamboat and would not embrace the new technology. The *Savannah* was sold to a commercial merchant, but within two years, it ran aground off of Long Island, New York, and broke into many pieces, never to sail again.

THE *GREAT EASTERN*

In the mid-nineteenth century, Isambard Kingdom Brunel suggested to the Eastern Steam Navigation Company in England that it build a giant steam-powered ship. At that time, the important and profitable Far East and Australia route was sailed by the fast clipper ships, but Brunel claimed that a

The *Great Eastern*, the first attempt at a large luxury steamship, used two 56-foot side-wheels and 10 boilers to propel its 680-foot-long iron hull with the power of steam. It took 2,000 workers four years, from 1854 to 1858, to construct the luxurious steamship on England's River Thames.

steam-powered ship could sail the route even faster. He was awarded the money and means to mastermind his gigantic steamship, which became known as the *Great Eastern*. Capable of carrying 4,000 passengers, the ship included six masts with sails used for backup power, two 56-foot side-wheels, and 10 boilers producing 2,600 horsepower. Inside were velvet parlor rooms for high-paying travelers. Chandeliers hung from the Grand Saloon ceiling and huge mirrors lined its walls. Furniture was handmade for high-class relaxation.

When Brunel came for the final inspection of his "great babe," he had a stroke due to the stress he had endured during the building of the monster ship. Then, in September 1858, disaster struck the *Great Eastern* on a trial run down the

English Channel when a massive explosion occurred in its hold. "There was a confused roar amid which came the awful crash of timber and iron mingled together in a frightful uproar, and then all was hidden in a rush of steam."[18] Once the steam cleared, it was discovered that 15 crewmen had been killed or injured.

The second attempt at a maiden voyage was set for June 16, 1860, for a route from Southampton, England, to New York City. This voyage caused quite a stir throughout the world. One newspaper reported that when "'the monster struck out for the New World, [it was] the first ocean voyage of a ship that has been the parent of more talk, speculation and wonder, and world-wide interest, than any craft since Noah's Ark.'"[19]

Unfortunately, the huge vessel had too many problems. Its luxurious rooms were never filled and it had accidents that were expensive to repair. The cost of building and repairing the ship bankrupted several companies.

In 1861, another disaster struck the *Great Eastern* when a storm tore off its steering shaft and paddle wheels. The boat tossed wildly in the churning sea, and in the Grand Saloon, passengers were struck by the tumbling furniture. In total, passengers and crew sustained 25 broken limbs during the storm.

Later, the *Great Eastern* was used to lay cable along the ocean floor. Ultimately, the first gigantic luxury cruise liner was made into a floating carnival by a Liverpool merchant.

A WAVE OF STEAM CRUISE LINERS

The *Great Eastern* inspired other shipbuilders with big ideas. A German, Albert Ballin, was determined to build the largest ship in the world. He was the owner of the Hamburg-America Line, which ran ocean liners to ferry European emigrants to the New World.

Ballin's only competition, the British Cunard Line, was in the process of building the *Aquitania*—slated to be the largest steam cruise liner in the world—when Ballin began building his *Vaterland* (German for "Fatherland"). Ballin was a perfectionist, and wanted every detail of his ship to be of the highest quality. While inspecting the ship, he would jot down such notes as, "'Toast to be served in a napkin—hot,'" "'Dirty-linen closet too small; butter dishes too small,'" and "'The pillows should be softer, plumper.'" [20]

Once the ship was completed in 1914, it required 900 crewmembers to service it. The ship also required an astronomical amount of coal to keep it sailing.

Prior to sailing, the ship was stocked with "13,800 table napkins, 6,870 tablecloths . . . 45,000 pounds of fresh meat and 24,000 pounds of canned and pickled meats; 100,000 pounds of potatoes; 10,000 pounds of sugar . . . and 17,500 bottles of wines, champagnes and brandies." [21]

Accommodations on the steam liners in the early twentieth century were divided into three sections: first class, second

Safety Aboard the Steamships

As early as 1840, trans-Atlantic shipbuilders were brainstorming for ideas on how to save passengers in case of a shipwreck. One idea was a tight-fitting rubber helmet with a glass eye opening and a tube inside to allow the person to breathe. Another concept was a floating metal ball that could hold up to 50 people. It had a railing along the side to stand on during fair weather and a crank inside that moved the ball through the water. Also proposed was a waterproof cylindrical suit with a domed helmet that was supposed to float its wearer to safety. Stored in the suit was a month's supply of food and water. None of these ideas were developed.

After the tragic sinking of the *Titanic*, strict laws were passed to ensure the safety of passengers during a disaster. All large ships had to be stocked with enough lifeboats to accommodate all the passengers. Prior to sailing, all passengers had to assemble for instruction on using the provided life jackets and assignment to a particular lifeboat.

class, and steerage class. First and second classes had access to beautifully designed dining rooms, exercise rooms, tiled swimming pools, a social hall, and comfortable cabins. Women would bring up to four changes of clothing a day for different activities, including ballroom dancing, deck tennis, miniature golf, swimming, and shows featuring cancan girls or boxing matches. There were even private kennels for the dogs of first-class passengers.

The majority of passengers were in the steerage class, which had narrow bunk beds and only two toilets for every 100 passengers. They ate basic meals with no frills and had access only to outside decks, which were used to store cargo. These passengers paid $50 for the trip to America, whereas first-class passengers paid $4,000.

Unfortunately, the fate of the *Vaterland* was dismal. After only seven Atlantic crossings, the ship was docked in New York City when World War 1 broke out. Rumors circulated that the departing *Vaterland* was taking German sympathizers back to Germany to fight against France and Great Britain, and the *Vaterland* was not allowed to leave the port. Tied to a pier, the ship's hull began to rust. Ballin was frustrated and heartbroken that his crowning achievement was coming to nothing. After being tied up for three years, the *Vaterland* was seized by the United States government.

Over the following years, there appeared other huge steam liners with names such as *Normandie, Titanic, Queen Mary,* and *Queen Elizabeth.* The engines on steam liners were massive. Depending on the ship, it could consist of two huge reciprocating engines—one used to drive the port (left-hand side) and one to drive the starboard (right-hand side) of the ship. Included was a 16,000 horsepower steam turbine driven by a four-blade propeller. Each of the reciprocating engines weighed up to 1,000 tons and stood up to 30 feet high. It took 162 furnaces to give these massive engines enough steam. The furnaces needed to be fed over 600 tons of coal per day and it

The USS *Leviathan,* seen here cruising into New York Harbor around 1925, was better known as the German steamship *Vaterland.* Once used to transport first-class passengers in fine style (and steerage passengers with only the barest necessities), the *Vaterland* was seized by the United States when World War I began.

took 160 men to do it. The elegant cruise ships of today owe their heritage to the inventive builders of these magnificent steam ships.

PERSONAL STORIES

Steamship passenger, poet, and author Robert Louis Stevenson, who traveled steerage class to New York, noted that, "In steerage there are males and females . . . but in second [class] (and naturally in first), passengers were regarded as ladies and gentlemen." [22]

Another writer, Ludwig Bemelmans, who traveled steerage class "objected to the vibration and pitching—and even more so to 'a man who had dirty finger-nails,' who sat with him at table." [23]

When the *Vaterland* was ready to sail, "A crowd of emigrants, shawls and caps protecting them from the drizzle, lined the rails and perched atop lifeboats . . . to wave farewell to friends. The departure . . . was so quiet . . . that many of the first-class passengers . . . in the dining saloon, were not even aware they were under way." [24]

The *Queen Mary* was a famous cruise liner. On it, "passengers were treated like royalty. Bags and trunks were whisked [away] by baggage handlers. . . . Each stateroom contained two comfortable single beds, a writing desk, and a small table with overstuffed chairs . . . The bathtub had hot and cold running salt water and fresh water . . . in the 1930s . . . many people enjoyed taking a saltwater bath." [25]

The steam liners ruled the seas, but on land many inventions were starting to pique the public's interest. Steam engines were increasingly being used to automate a wide range of land-based vehicles.

5 Advancements in Steam Technology

The powerful steam engine raised society's expectations about technology. People and goods needed to be quickly transported overland. Demand for standardized products was extremely high. Factories needed to increase the speed at which they made their products. Large-scale farming needed to be established to feed the factory workers living in the towns and cities. How was all this to be done?

In the eighteenth century, steam power jumped from the stationary steam engine to an engine that could drive a machine. The door opened to many new possibilities. Inventors developing different modes of transportation used their imaginations to come up with new and sometimes bizarre machines. Several vehicles we use today were first developed in the mid-nineteenth century in response to the power of steam.

LAND STEAM VEHICLES

In 1769, a Frenchman named Nicolas Cugnot built a steam-powered wooden carriage with three wheels that could travel two to three miles per hour. A large, kettle-type boiler hung in the front, and the driver had to stop and fill it with water every 15 minutes.

William Murdock also developed a steam-powered vehicle. Murdock was proud of his invention and liked to drive it around his village. One night, after lighting a lamp to illuminate his way as he drove, he passed a church. "The parson happened to see the model and, thinking it was the devil

Nicolas Cugnot's Steam Road Carriage was propelled by steam generated in the combination stove and kettle at the vehicle's front. Travel by the steam carriage was considerably slow — not only did it travel at two to three miles per hour, but the driver also had to stop and fill the kettle with water every 15 minutes.

himself breathing fire, fled in panic from the churchyard." [26]

Later to be known as the "Father of the Locomotive," Richard Trevithick also built a steam carriage. When Trevithick's cousin test-drove it on a road, one of the wheels got stuck in a deep rut, causing the vehicle to fall on its side. All the passengers hopped out and went to a tavern for a meal. Meanwhile, the carriage caught fire and was completely destroyed.

Trevithick went on to make another steam-powered carriage. This one did not fare much better: Troublesome steering caused the vehicle to crash. Trevithick then turned his attention to rail travel.

These steam-powered carriages inspired the inventors of the Stanley Steamer. The Stanley twins, Francis and Freelan, first produced this automobile in 1897. By 1898, they had built three Stanley Steamers. The steamers received a lot of attention when

William Murdock

William Murdock's contributions to the advancement of the steam engine are not as well known as Watt's, probably because Murdock was Watt's employee. When Murdock joined Boulton and Watt in 1777, the quick learner proved to be hardworking and reliable. Watt saw Murdock's potential and requested his assistance in developing the sun and planet gear.

While in Boulton and Watt's employ, Murdock worked on his own inventions, which included a modification to Watt's steam engine. He experimented with rotating steam engines, one of which he used for a moving carriage.

After Watt retired, his sons offered a partnership to Murdock, which he happily accepted. Murdock went on to patent some of his own ideas, including a new type of valve that controlled the flow of steam to a cylinder. It later became known as the D-slide valve because its sliding door was shaped like the letter D. This valve remained in use for over 100 years.

the twins drove them around Cambridge, Massachusetts, which led to the twins' first sale of a car in Boston. Within a year, the Stanleys had manufactured 200 Stanley Steamers.

The Stanley Steamer was appealing because there was little vibration in the vehicle and the motor was very quiet. It could reach speeds of 55 to 60 miles per hour, at least 15 miles per hour faster than the speediest gasoline automobile of the time. The engine's water was heated by kerosene, and the radiator acted as the steam condenser.

The steam engine was not the best engine to use while traveling by road because they were extremely heavy, needed a skilled driver, and it took too much time to power up the steam. Also, there was always the possibility that the boiler would blow up. One of the advantages of the steam engine, however, was that it accelerated much faster than a gas-powered engine.

The Stanley brothers' vehicle caught the attention of magazine publisher John B. Walker, who asked them how much they wanted for their company. They named what was then an exorbitant amount — $250,000 — thinking that Walker could not afford it. To their surprise, Walker immediately paid the sum and they were without a company.

The Stanley brothers soon formed another company and continued making cars through the early twentieth century. However, they were hit hard when the gasoline engine began to take over the car engine market. By 1925, the Stanley brothers had filed for bankruptcy and were out of business.

Public buses powered by steam started to replace horse-drawn public transportation by the late nineteenth century. The average person could not afford to purchase a car, and buses provided an alternative to train travel.

One steam bus called the Automaton was made in 1836. Its engine and boiler were in the rear of the vehicle, and it could carry up to 22 passengers. In England, another steam bus was called the "woodie bus" because there was wood on its sides. These buses transported paying passengers throughout England on scheduled, fixed routes.

Steam trucks developed in the 1920s were used to transport goods and haul dirt and rocks from construction sites. One truck even had a bed that tilted back to dump its cargo onto the ground.

Bicycles early on were fitted with steam engines, giving birth to the motorcycle. In 1867, S.H. Roper in the United States invented the first steam-powered bicycle. Roper took his steam-powered bike to fairs and circuses to give demonstrations. At about the same time in Paris, Pierre and Ernest Michaux were busy building steam-powered bikes of their own. In the Michaux model, the steam engine was fitted beneath the seat of the bicycle. The model reached speeds of 19 miles per hour. Soon, powered bicycles were speeding along city streets.

The power of steam was also employed to fight fires. Londoners John Ericsson and John Braithwaite developed

This first motorized bicycle was steam-powered. Built by S. H. Roper in 1867, the steam engine was positioned underneath a raised seat. A precursor to the motorcycles driven today, the steam-powered bicycle could reach speeds of up to 19 miles per hour.

the first steam-pump fire engine in 1829. A steam engine was attached to the back of a horse-drawn carriage. When the fire alarm sounded at the fire station, the firemen would throw burning coals into the firebox below the boiler on the carriage. The horses were brought out of their stalls and hooked up to the carriage. Whipping the strong horses, the firemen raced through town to the scene of the fire, one man driving the carriage and another riding behind, stoking the fire. By the time they arrived, the steam engine was heated up and ready to go. Once the 1,000-foot-long leather hose was hooked up to a water source such as a stream, river, or well, it could spray water up to 29 feet in the air and throw it a distance of 180 feet. By 1850, steam fire engines were used in many large cities. Later, gasoline-powered cabs instead of horses pulled the engines.

STEAM ON THE FARM

From 1890 to 1920, steam traction engines, the predecessors of gas tractors, became very popular. They could plow a farmer's field in half the time it took using horses. Plow horses eventually tired and needed to rest. The farmer then had a choice: He could either switch to fresh horses if he had more, or he could wait until the animals were rested. Steam traction engines, however, could run all day, as long as there were water and fuel.

Most farmers could not afford to purchase a steam traction engine, which cost anywhere from $600 to $3,000. The average yearly salary at this time was $400. Instead, farmers would hire a team to thresh and plow that brought their own steam traction engine, equipment, steam engineer, and work crew. These teams would go from farm to farm and charge a set fee. This worked out well for the farmers, because very few of them understood how to run a steam engine or how to fix it if it broke down. Instead, the engineer kept the engine running smoothly and served as the mechanic if necessary.

It sometimes took two men to drive a single tractor. One drove while the other refueled the boiler with wood or coal and watched the gauges. Traction engines carried their own limited supplies of wood and water. To work continuously, horse-drawn wagons carrying fuel and water had to resupply them. The boiler was refueled by a worker called a stoker, who opened a heavy metal door and threw the wood or coal into a large and very hot fire.

Encased in a thick jacket of metal around the fire was the boiler water. The boiler was heavily built to withstand the pressure of steam and boiling water, which could get up to 150 pounds per square inch or more. The boiler would get very hot on the outside too, easily reaching 330 degrees Fahrenheit

At a price between $600 and $3,000, most farmers could not afford to buy a steam traction engine to plow their fields. Instead, they hired a team that owned a plow and an engine like this one at the Thomas Ranch in Chico, California.

(166 degrees Celsius). The engineer and stoker could be badly burned by accidentally touching the boiler walls. Sometimes water leaked from the pipes, sizzling and spitting as it landed on the boiler.

The engineer had to drive very carefully because there were no brakes on steam traction engines, even though they weighed several tons. Usually, the only way to stop was to roll slowly until the large machine came to a halt.

To announce that the machine was coming, the engineer would pull back on a chain, opening up a loud, sharp steam whistle much like those used on locomotives. The whistle was an important part of the engine. It was also used to signal to the work crew to bring water or fuel, take a lunch break, or look out for danger.

Steam traction engines could also be used as stationary work engines. Belts could be attached to the engine's flywheel to drive threshers, which separated the grain from the straw, cornshellers, which separated the corn kernels from the cob, and other farm machinery.

Steam traction engines were built for heavy work and proved to be extremely durable. Many can be seen running today at steam shows and threshing bees after being carefully restored by today's steam-engine enthusiasts.

THE STATIONARY STEAM ENGINE

Although the horizontal and rotating steam engines had been invented, the stationary vertical engine was in no way considered obsolete. Throughout the eighteenth century, it was made in different sizes and shapes and became an all-purpose engine. It could be hooked up via wheels, pulleys, and belts to power threshing machines, sawmills, water pumps, air compressors, and gristmills. The piston could be positioned vertically or horizontally, depending on its use. Stationary steam engines even powered colorful musical carousels at fairs.

Factories and mills used the stationary engine as a means of powering many other devices as well. At one end of a factory, a huge boiler connected to a stationary steam engine would be fed constantly to keep the steam at a high pressure. The engine's piston was attached to a connecting rod, which turned a crankshaft to change the piston's linear motion into a circular motion. The crankshaft was attached to a flywheel, to which belts were attached to provide power to one or more devices.

The engineers of these large steam engines had to very carefully watch all the gauges. They had to check the pressure gauge to make sure there wasn't too much pressure, and they had to check the water gauge to make sure there was enough water to run the machine. Although the boilers were equipped with a variety of safety devices, accidents did occasionally occur, and when they did, they were devastating. One such accident occurred about 120 years ago. A steam boiler blew up, killing nine men and shaking the city of Canton, Ohio, early one Saturday morning. Accidents involving boilers were not uncommon in the 1800s, before metallurgy, the science of metals, was well understood. By the 1890s, however, boilers were much heavier and safer to use.

STEAM POWER IN THE AIR

The first man to attempt air travel with a steam engine was Clement Ader, a French inventor. He built a single-wing plane powered with a steam engine that in 1890 flew for a distance of 165 feet, although he was just eight inches off the ground.

Four years later, an American, Hiram Maxim, wealthy from inventing the Maxim machine gun, turned his attention to air travel. He created a huge plane called a biplane for its two sets of wings, one above the other. Two steam engines on the biplane turned the two large propellers.

Maxim was sure that his plane would become airborne, but didn't know how he would control it once it was in the air. To test this problem, he made his plane fly along rails 1,800 feet long. On July 31, 1894, Maxim and his crew took the plane up into the air. It lifted so violently that the plane crashed and was badly damaged. Maxim later lost interest in his airplane experiments.

George and William Besler were the first to develop a working steam engine airplane. They worked on it for three years and first tested it publicly at Oakland Airport, California, in 1934. The Besler brothers took the plane up three times, to the amazement of the watching crowd.

Landing was much more efficient using a steam engine. The pilot pulled back on a lever and the propeller at the front of the plane immediately reversed and whirled backward. This proved to be a very effective braking mechanism that allowed the plane to stop quickly.

The steam engine was located at the front of the plane. It

George and William Besler developed the first working steam engine airplane in the early 1830s. In this photograph of the Beslers' plane, George Besler is nearly obscured in the pilot's seat by the steam issuing from the engine.

had to be fed water constantly through a device called a steam donkey pump. Ten gallons of water were sufficient to fly the plane for 400 miles.

The steam-powered plane was extremely quiet when it was in the air, making it easy for passengers to converse. In fact, the pilot could even call to people on the ground below and be heard.

PERSONAL STORIES

Mrs. Prescott Warren was the daughter of Francis Stanley, one of the inventors of the Stanley Steamer. She recalls the first time she drove it: "I grasped the tiller, put the power on, tried out the foot brake, found it worked, and got underway. It was just like riding

Early steam-pump fire engines were pulled by horses. When the alarm sounded, the firemen threw burning coals in the engine's firebox to heat the boiler. By the time the truck arrived at the fire, the steam pump was ready to spray water 180 feet from the end of the hose and up to 29 feet in the air.

a bicycle, only easier . . . I believe it marks the first time a woman ever drove a steam car. I was thrilled to death!" [27]

She drove the steam car several times and recalled being stopped by a policeman. "I was going ten or twelve miles an hour . . . and he blew his whistle at me. He ordered me to stop and told me that I was violating the speed limit!" [28]

In 1906, a Stanley Steamer broke the land speed record. The "Rocket," driven by Fred Marriott, reached a peak speed of 127.659 miles per hour.

The next year, Marriott tried to break that world record. He recounted what happened: "I shouldn't have tried to shatter all records . . . She wasn't heavy enough. I thought I could make her do two hundred. But that confounded combination of speed, light weight and treacherous sand spun me around, shot me eighteen feet in the air. It was the last time I ever raced a car." [29]

One man, Jack Johnson, recalled watching fire drills as a child. The firehouse in his town had several steam-engine fire trucks that were pulled by horses. "Firemen would come . . . sliding down the shiny brass pole. At the same instant the bars to the stalls would raise and the beautiful horses would come clopping out at a brisk trot. Each . . . would take his place beneath a suspended harness in front of the steam engine." [30]

Johnson said that the horses would be ready to go in just a few minutes. They would stomp their feet and toss their heads in anticipation of running to the scene of the fire. When the drill ended, the harnesses were taken off and the watching children were allowed to come in and pet the beloved animals.

6

The Steam Locomotive

AT ISSUE

Boats and ships were the most economical ways to move products and goods in the late nineteenth century. But if a city or town was not near water, how could it be supplied with food and other goods needed for its citizens' survival?

Most large cities and towns were established by canals or rivers because of this very problem. Packhorses, oxen, and mules pulled wagons hauling animal furs, cloth, and grain to towns established far inland. The trip could take weeks, months, sometimes even years. How could this process be speeded up? Because of this evident need for a machine to expedite overland shipping, inventors turned their attention to developing a hauling vehicle that could travel on land. That vehicle was later known as the locomotive. The era of the railroads was about to begin.

RICHARD TREVITHICK

By 1804, the steam engine was being used to move carriages on land and boats on water. Richard Trevithick, a steam engineer, turned his attention to creating a rail locomotive.

The idea of using rails for roads came up as early as the Roman era. They laid down flat slabs of stone for wheels to turn on. Later, wooden planks were tried, but the wheels slipped off the planks too easily, hindering travel. Their solution was to make a rim called a flange on the inner side of the wheel. The rim fit snuggly against the side of the plank, keeping the wheel on it. Eventually, an iron wheel on an iron track was found to create the least amount of resistance.

Deemed the "Father of the Locomotive" for a train engine he built in 1804, steam engineer Richard Trevithick built another locomotive that he called *Catch-me-who-can* in 1808. Trevithick pioneered the idea of using steam-powered machines on rails. He charged the London public a small fee to ride around a circular track in a carriage pulled by the engine.

The gauge—the distance between the rails of the track—was also established in the Roman era. Roman chariots wore deep grooves into the ground as they traveled over the roads. Later, stagecoaches were built with their wheels the same distance apart to match the grooves in the existing roads. Then, when trains were first built and tracks started to be laid, the same gauge was chosen to accommodate some of the first train cars, which were converted stagecoaches.

Prior to locomotives, some stagecoaches were fitted with iron wheels and run on routes laid with iron tracks. These routes were in service until the locomotive replaced the horse as a source of power for transportation.

During the Industrial Revolution, tramways or lines of connected wagons took coal from the mines to the nearest canals or rivers for shipping. Originally, horses drew these wagons, but as the demand for coal increased, the wooden tracks kept wearing out. Finally the idea of using iron for the tracks became a reality, but horses were still needed to pull the loads. Steam power was the logical solution, so Trevithick made the first steam-powered locomotive in 1804. "It is reputed to have pulled five wagons loaded with ten tons of iron and seventy men; however it broke the cast-iron plate tramway in a number of places. Rather than re-lay the track with stronger plates the owners reverted to horse power." [31]

Later, in 1808, Trevithick constructed a locomotive called *Catch-me-who-can*. He placed it on a circular train track and charged a small fee for passengers to ride in an attached coach.

GEORGE STEPHENSON

In 1812, steam-powered wagons were being used to transport coal in England. During this time, a skilled mechanic, George Stephenson, and his son Robert created a locomotive that did not transfer the power of the steam engine to the locomotive's wheels via gears and beams. Instead, power went directly from the engine to a connecting rod attached to a piston that turned the wheels of the locomotive. This was a major achievement in locomotive development. The father-and-son team built a dozen different locomotives to transport coal and later estab-lished the first firm with the purpose of building locomotives, Robert Stephenson and Company.

The Liverpool & Manchester Railway hired the Stephenson company to make a steam locomotive, and the father and son built one to which they attached several luxurious cars.

Members of the British royalty were invited to be the first passengers. On September 13, 1830, crowds appeared to watch the locomotive's inaugural run, during which it reached speeds of 15 to 25 miles per hour. Although the Liverpool & Manchester was not the first railway in England, it became known as the Grand British Experimental Railway.

UNITED STATES RAILWAY

Steam-powered locomotives did not go unnoticed in the United States. The Baltimore and Ohio Railroad Company was established in 1827, but tracks were laid all the way to Ohio not until 24 years later. A 13-mile train track was laid and various small locomotives were used such as the *Tom Thumb*, which had a one-horsepower engine and could haul 36 people at up to 18 miles per hour. States such as South Carolina and New York also laid train tracks and began to experiment with their own locomotives.

Meanwhile, in 1829, the first full-size locomotive came to the United States. A New York engineer, Horatio Allen, imported it from England. Shortly thereafter, railway lines sprang up throughout the East Coast. By 1840, there were 2,818 miles of tracks. Only 20 years later, it had increased to 30,626 miles of laid track. The East Coast rail system became the busiest and most congested in the world.

The public was at first skeptical and resistant to the idea of a steam locomotive. The general belief was that "a horse was more reliable, consumed local fuel, [and] did not require trained mechanics . . . There were doctors who asserted that the high speeds which the steam locomotives might attain must be injurious, if not fatal." [32]

The idea was even rejected by the religious clergy. They preached that "in the steam locomotive man was rashly trying to imprison the devil. It was the devil's efforts to escape that created

The Baltimore and Ohio Railroad Company built a 13-mile stretch of track between two stations and used locomotives like the *Tom Thumb* (seen here) to haul passengers and goods. This small engine was the first steam locomotive built in America and the first, on August 28, 1830, to pull a load of passengers.

all the noise, heat and steam, caused the pistons to move to and fro, and might end in tearing the boiler apart." [33]

Once railways were built and trains began to be more prevalent, signals were developed to communicate with the locomotive engineer. Men were appointed to stand next to the tracks and wave a flag in a particular way depending on the message, which could be "all clear," "caution," or "slacken speed." The flagmen were later replaced with tall poles having wooden flags extending horizontally at the top. A man below could change the positions of the flags to relay a message to the engineer.

Before the Civil War, the northeastern United States had many railroad tracks and trains in operation, but the South did not have as many rail resources. The North's ability to move men and materials quickly by rail assisted them in winning the Civil War.

After the war, railroads were built at a rapid speed across the Great Plains. Soon, railroads replaced rivers as the primary means of moving passengers and goods from one place to another. Farming communities and small towns sprouted up beside these new tracks, and huge wooden trestles were built to allow passage across rivers and deep valleys.

RIDING THE TRAIN

The geography of the United States presented unique problems for rail travel. In Europe, fences were built along the train tracks to keep animals out of the way. The United States was so vast, however, that building and maintaining fences alongside the tracks were tasks that no one cared to undertake. One of the problems was the enormous herds of buffalo that roamed the prairie. Sometimes these herds would graze beside or on the tracks. To clear the way, a locomotive would eject a burst of steam from a pipe in the front, surprising and frightening the beasts into quickly moving off the tracks. Some passengers traveled with the sole purpose of shooting buffalo. Rifles lined the luggage racks, and when the train passed a herd of buffalo, passengers would open the windows and shoot at the grazing animals as the train whizzed by. Sometimes the train would even stop to accommodate the shooters.

When traveling by train, it could take passengers many days to get to their destination. If the inside of the car became too stuffy or confining for the weary passengers, they could simply walk back to the rear car and climb the ladder to sit atop the train in the open air.

On the front of the locomotive was a V-shaped grill called a cowcatcher that pushed aside anything that was blocking the tracks, such as cows (dead or alive), boulders, fallen trees, and snow. Sometimes passengers rode on the cowcatcher from town to town.

Early trains derailed so frequently that "some early railway tickets included a clause to the effect that passengers were liable to help put the engines or cars back on the track again." [34]

Tragedies on the Railroad

The world's first train crash happened between Versailles and Paris, France, on May 8, 1842. The train derailed and then caught on fire. All the passengers were locked in the train's cars and 57 people were killed. Unfortunately, other accidents followed, such as the one in 1868 that involved an Irish train loaded with petroleum. It crashed, and in the ensuing fire, 33 passengers burned to death. Another train in the British Isles in 1879 was crossing a tall bridge when a defect in the bridge's design caused it to collapse during a violent windstorm. The train fell headlong into the water below. None of the 80 people aboard survived.

Collisions between trains caused the most deaths. Sometimes, engineers were forced by dense fog to slow down or even stop their trains and were rear-ended by the train behind them. Later, a train employee was appointed to warn the engineer of the train behind to stop.

Some engineers were bullheaded and would not back down for an oncoming train on the same track. Instead, they chose to run head-on into the approaching locomotive. Threats of dismissal and arrest warrants quickly put an end to this practice.

Head-on collisions occurred for other reasons as well. Early switching systems had problems, and sometimes two trains headed toward each other were switched onto the same track. Other train wrecks were caused by poorly built or decaying bridges that collapsed, wooden passenger cars catching fire from the kerosene lamps inside, and boilers blowing up.

Railways developed a reputation for being careless with passengers' lives, but no group suffered more deaths and injuries than those who worked on

As train travel grew in popularity, more and more passengers boarded. One of the problems facing these rail travelers was the lack of a timetable. It was difficult to tell when a train would arrive at or depart from a particular location. Also, there were no set depots at which passengers could board trains. In cities, trains ran through the center of town and stopped at certain street corners. In the country, however, trains sometimes seemed to stop for no apparent reason. If someone needed to board, he or she could flag down the

Along with the wonders of train travel came the horrors of accidents, such as this derailment. Railway companies were accused of being careless with their passengers' lives, but casualties among their own employees were far greater in number.

the railway. "In 1888, . . . 315 passengers were killed, 2,138 injured; 2,070 employees were killed and 20,148 injured."*

* Ogburn, Charlton. *Railroads: The Great American Adventure.* Washington, D.C.: National Geographic Society, 1977, p. 98.

The first passenger trains were stagecoaches equipped with railroad wheels pulled by a steam locomotive. The coaches' backless wooden seats and low roofs were so uncomfortable that they prompted George M. Pullman to develop his Pullman Sleeper cars, which made it possible for travelers to ride in comfort.

engineer by waving a brightly colored shirt or cloth. The engineer might ignore the request and carry on with the journey or stop the train to allow the person to board.

The first railroad cars were stagecoach bodies fitted with railroad wheels. The seats were wooden planks with no back and the roof was so low that passengers had to stoop while walking down the aisle. Even though there were improvements such as straight-back seats, rail travel was far from comfortable. George M. Pullman, seeing the need for a change, developed the Pullman Sleeper. This was a car outfitted with beds with sheets and blankets, washrooms with running water, and dining carts with white linen tablecloths, china, and silverware.

As rail travel continued to expand into cities throughout the country, the tracks were laid in busy streets. Walking through town could prove dangerous if close attention was not paid to approaching locomotives.

Trains traveling in the West often had to carry armed soldiers to protect their cargo. In the early days of train travel, shipments of gold and other valuables attracted train robbers and other villains. Battles frequently were fought over the precious items.

The most famous train robbers were Jesse James and his gang. "In 1873, when Jesse robbed his first train, he derailed the locomotive and the engineer died in the crash—the first of many railroad workers and other victims killed by the James gang." [35]

One of the most important railway employees was the engineer. Early engineers were very highly regarded in their communities, and they often wore top hats and ties to accentuate their status. Their ability to run the huge, steaming locomotives verged on magic in the eyes of most people.

Engineers took great pride in their engines, even decorating their locomotives for the holidays. At Christmastime, often the front and sides of an engine would be hung with holly and berries, giving it a festive air. For everyday use, the interiors of many cars had cushioned seats (some covered in velvet), large clocks, and linoleum flooring.

The largely unseen firemen were responsible for keeping the fire going. Sooty-faced and sweating, they doggedly shoveled wood or coal into the blazing firebox. Coal and water were stored in a car called a tender that was attached behind the locomotive. In the early days, the firemen had to use big scoop shovels to fuel the furnace. Later, mechanical stokers that fed the coal into the fire were developed. Even so, the firemen still had to adjust the stoker, monitor the water level and add more if needed, and troubleshoot engine problems.

Better known was the train boy, who hopped aboard when the train pulled into a town to sell popular items like coffee, tea, sugar, fruits, soaps, and towels. Passengers eagerly flagged him down to purchase supplies. A successful train boy could make $80 in a week, an enormous sum given that a conductor earned only $60 a month.

The conductor was a very notable figure on board the train. Not only did he sell and collect tickets, he also was known to expand his duties to include serving as a matchmaker for likely couples, settling arguments among the passengers, disciplining rowdy children, and scolding drunkards.

PROMONTORY SUMMIT

One of the greatest feats in the railroad history of the United States was connecting the Central Pacific Railroad to the Union Pacific Railroad, thus providing service from coast to coast. Human muscle power and large draft animals were employed to lay the tracks. Men were paid $1.25 to $1.50 a day and given a bed to sleep in and food to eat. In return, they cleared the route of obstacles, built the roadbed, and then placed the huge wooden beams called ties on the roadbed. Heavy iron rails were then laid on the ties and spiked to secure the tracks. These workforces were so large they were like little cities. When winter's bitterly cold winds blew, towns sprang up, some as large as 7,000 men, where the workers were waiting out the weather. Fights broke out among the inhabitants, most likely from the mind-numbing boredom.

During the working months, some Native Americans, unhappy about the Iron Horse, as the locomotive was called, screaming through their prairie homelands, raided camps and killed workers. Even after the tracks were laid, tribes continued to fight against the Iron Horse. They derailed trains and sometimes scalped passengers. Finally, they accepted

On May 10, 1869, the directors of the Central Pacific and Union Pacific railways shook hands and drove a golden spike into the ground at Promontory Summit, Utah, to mark the completion of the Transcontinental Railroad. The project connected the country, allowing passengers and goods to travel from one coast of the United States to the other by rail.

the "bad medicine wagon" [36] and moved north, following the wandering buffalo.

In 1869, the Central Pacific and Union Pacific lines met at Promontory Summit, Utah. This formed the transcontinental rail link. Men cheered and waved their hats as the two lines' directors shook hands and hammered in a golden spike to represent the uniting of the country by the railroad, which stretched from the Atlantic Ocean to the Pacific Ocean. The entire nation celebrated the magnificent achievement. At City Hall Park in New York, a hundred guns fired a salute and bells clanged in celebration at Independence Hall in Philadelphia.

Steam locomotives appeared in countries throughout the world: Australia, New Zealand, India, Kenya, France, Belgium, and Germany, to name a few. Great Britain continued to be on the cutting edge of railroad technology. In 1863, construction of the first underground railway was begun to allow quick and easy passage throughout London. This underground rail service became known as the "tube" in modern London and the "subway" in the United States.

Steam locomotives have been phased out in many countries and replaced by diesel or electric trains. Other countries, however, such as Kenya, Zimbabwe, Zambia, China, and India, still use steam locomotives today.

PERSONAL STORIES

Early trains were not known for their comfort. A passenger remarked that it was "'only remarkable for [its] extreme plainness . . . [a] long, narrow wooden box, like a flat-roofed Noah's ark.' At one end of the car a wood-burning stove stood on a tiny platform. An enclosed space at the other end held the toilet, which was referred to as the 'convenience.'" [37]

Later, upper-class American travelers only wanted to travel in first-class Pullman cars. William Dean Howells, a writer, observed, "[Americans] surveyed with infinite satisfaction the elegance of the flying parlor in which they sat. . . . They said that none but Americans or enchanted princes in the Arabian Nights ever traveled in such state." [38]

Train cars were converted into hunting lodges and pulled behind the other cars. In 1876, Jerome Marble rented a car that was outfitted for the perfect hunting vacation on the Dakota prairie with gun cases, refrigerators for freshly killed game, and kennels for dogs.

Rail lines featured top passenger services, as one traveler recalled of the Chicago-to-New Orleans *Panama Limited.* "'The *Panama* attained its glory because of its luxurious accommodations and the great care exerted in the dining car. They put on an elaborate feast called the King's Dinner. It included Gulf shrimps, crabmeat—six or seven courses. . . .'" [39]

7

The Steam Engine and the Industrial Age

AT ISSUE

During the Industrial Revolution, factories, textile mills, and massive mines reshaped the environment and lifestyles in England, continental Europe, and the United States. Industrial factories powered by steam engines doubled and then quadrupled the amount of goods produced.

The nineteenth century saw the first use of steam locomotives and trains and the first tracks being laid. This allowed people to settle comfortably away from the city. Steam liners sailed around the world. Passengers traveled in unprecedented comfort and style.

The development of the steam engine in the eighteenth century spurred inventors to make machines more efficient and productive. As machines replaced muscle power, the general population wanted speedier production and delivery of goods and more entertainment.

But there were also such problems and issues as safe and fair working conditions and child labor. In addition, the innovations completely changed the rules of war.

THE STEAM ENGINE AND TRANSPORTATION

Prior to the development of the steam engine, the majority of trade occurred by utilizing seaports and harbors along large rivers. Thus, geography determined what areas of the world would be the most heavily populated. Roads in the early nineteenth century were nothing more than wide dirt paths through the forests. To enable rivers to be crossed, either bridges were built or ferries were established to carry travelers. All roads led to villages along waterways.

The cost of moving goods overland was astronomical. Strong wagons pulled by teams of six horses or oxen carried the heavy loads.

As time passed, man-made canals and waterways were dug to allow access to inland areas. England and other European countries constructed many of these canals. They were mainly used during the eighteenth century into the nineteenth century to help transport goods during the Industrial Revolution. Canals worked well for transporting goods, but not all areas had canals. As an 1816 report from the United States Senate Committee stated, "A coal mine . . . may exist in the United States not more than 10 miles from valuable ores of iron and other materials, and both of them be useless until a canal is established between them, as the price of land carriage is too great to be borne by either." [40]

From 1815 to 1860, steamboats became the primary mode of transportation. Canals, rivers, and lakes were the perfect highways on which to operate them. In the valley of the Mississippi River, steamboats brought the Industrial Revolution to the area. "No section of the country was so completely dependent upon steam for effective transportation, and in no other part of the world were so many steamboats built and operated." [41]

However, once railroad tracks began to be laid throughout the United States and Europe, rail travel became the most desirable form of transportation. It was usually much faster and more dependable than steamboat travel. Trains operated throughout the year, whereas steamboats had to shut down for the winter because rivers and lakes would often freeze. Another advantage of trains was that passengers could buy one ticket that allowed them to transfer from train to train to reach their destination. Steamboat companies were not as well organized, and passengers had to purchase new tickets for each leg of the trip.

Because the United States included such vast amounts of land, it needed a fast, cheap, and flexible mode of transportation. The most revolutionary invention of the time, the railroad, filled that need. It quickly and dependably transported goods and

The steam locomotive provided the means to transport many new Americans to cities and towns throughout the United States, sometimes in such large numbers that the passengers had to ride in cattle cars. These Dutch immigrants, photographed in 1910, were among the many immigrants who traveled by train to settle in the Midwest.

people on overland routes. Although the locomotive was first invented in England, railroads had their most dramatic growth in the United States: "By 1840, all [of] Europe had 1,818 miles of railroad; the United States, about 3,000." [42]

The railroads transported newly arrived immigrants to cities and small towns throughout the United States. Sometimes the trains were filled to capacity and as many passengers as possible were stuffed into open-air cattle cars. Even then, some passengers could find no space in the car and clung to the bars on the side of the car as the train sped along.

Mail delivery was also greatly improved. The steam engine made it possible for mail to be handled in a much faster and more consistent manner. Prior to the steam engine, mail could take months or even years to arrive at a faraway destination, if it arrived at all. Drivers of stagecoaches were sometimes frustrated by the weight of the mailbags and dumped the bags on the prairie.

Steamships speeded up ocean transportation. Between 1848 and 1860, the number of steamships built and in service grew enormously due to increased foreign trade. The popularity of steamships did not put sailing ships out of business, but the fact that steamships could cross the Atlantic Ocean in almost half the time it took sailing ships to cross meant that steamers carried the first-class passengers, mail, and high-fare freight. Sailing ships attracted only low-fare immigrant traffic and cumbersome freight.

Even though the steamship was considered the more desirable mode of travel, sailing ships continued to flourish because of their economical rates and empty hulls for shipping bulky, large freight. Most of the space in steamers' storage areas was needed for the coal to power the ship. Also, these large steamers required large staffs to maintain and repair the ship. It wasn't until the invention of the airplane that the sailing ships started to disappear.

MANUFACTURING WITH STEAM POWER

By the end of the eighteenth century, many types of industrial factories and mills, including mines, flour mills, oil mills, iron-works, and breweries, used steam engines. The use of the engine spread in the early nineteenth century to include printing and papermaking. This also included printing presses, which were powered by steam engines to print newspapers. Textile mills also employed the steam engine. "The making of fur and woolen hats, previously a time-consuming hand industry, was largely mechanized by 1860. . . . The sewing machine, invented by Elias Howe in 1846 . . . was rapidly introduced into the clothing and shoe trade during the fifties . . . They did work of an excellence impossible by hand methods." [43]

Steam engines needed replacement parts made of iron, and iron mills sprang up all over the United States as their use became more prevalent.

THE STEAM ENGINE IN WAR

The steam engine claimed its place in history as a commercial tool. It powered ships, cars, tractors, and trains. During the heyday of the engine's use, the world fought two major wars: World Wars I and II. The steam engine's primary use shifted from millwork and transportation to powering war machines. Civilian trains were converted to carry army troops. The huge luxury steam liners were gutted and converted into war ships.

The *Queen Mary* was one of those ships. During World War II, the signature black-and-white ship was repainted a dull gray to camouflage it. It often sailed alone. Because of its speed and ability to travel in stealth, it was nicknamed the Gray Ghost. The decks were fitted with anti-aircraft guns and special sonar-detection equipment was installed to detect submarines. Its luxurious berths were ripped out and replaced with bunk beds to sleep 5,000 men. The elegant bars were converted into medical stations. The *Queen Mary*'s purpose during World War II was to transport troops all over the world.

The ship zigzagged across the ocean to evade enemy ships, for it was in constant danger of torpedo attack. One close call occurred in Rio de Janeiro, Brazil. German spies who saw the *Queen Mary* refueling radioed the time of its departure to a waiting German submarine. The spies were captured and the captain of the *Queen Mary* was warned of the threat. Instead of leaving at the scheduled time, the captain left several hours earlier, so the *Queen Mary* got away safely. Another large tanker leaving Rio de Janeiro was not so lucky, however. As it departed, the German submarines torpedoed it.

Railroads have been extremely important in war since the American Civil War began in 1861. The South's Confederates used the railroad to obtain supplies. They were the first to turn railroad cars into ambulances. They also mounted guns on the train cars and attacked the North's railroad tracks and trains. However, maintaining railroads was no small undertaking, for locomotives had to be repaired and rotted tracks and worn-out

The *Queen Mary,* once a luxury steam liner, transported thousands of U.S. troops during World War II. It is pictured here steaming into New York Harbor on June 20, 1945, just two months before the end of the war. After the government painted the once sleek black-and-white ship gray, it earned the nickname "the Gray Ghost" for its speed and stealth.

iron wheels on the cars needed to be replaced. The majority of America's factories were located in the North, so for the Union, this was not a significant problem. The South, however, had few means of making parts for replacements. When the North blockaded the Southern ports, there was no way to import these necessary items, either.

Later, in World War I, railcars were also used as ambulances. They were stripped and fitted out with bunk beds, three beds high. Leather loops were attached to the ceiling for the injured soldiers to hang on to when the train jerked to a halt or started up.

The Germans put heavy cannons known as howitzers on their railcars. One howitzer called Big Bertha could launch a shell that would fall 70 miles away a little more than two minutes later. This cannon's aim was highly inaccurate.

During World War II, railways and stations were often the targets of heavy bombing. To protect locomotives, they were covered with armor plating and painted to camouflage them. However, railroad tracks often were heavily damaged and trains would be out of commission for several weeks while repairs were made.

Trains were even used to protect civilians. In London, children were ordered to report to the train station to be taken out of London for protection from a German attack. "Schoolchildren had to turn up in good order, in entire classes or groups under the supervision of teachers. At the stations all evacuees were to receive free railway tickets. They were to be carried by rail 50–80 kilometers [31–50 miles] from the capital in various directions." [44]

The Germans in World War II used trains not only in the fight, but also to transport over six million Jews and several million non-Jews to their deaths in concentration camps.

WORKING CONDITIONS IN FACTORIES

Along with expansion, the Industrial Age also brought its own set of problems, including how to treat workers and how to establish rules for an organization.

Society had changed so much that the lessons of the past no longer applied. Transportation had improved with steamboats and railway systems, and mass production of standardized products became the norm. Once factories were established, people left the home and went into the workplace to earn their living.

Workers and their rights had never before been considered. It became necessary to define what was right and what was wrong in the workplace, especially when dealing with children.

At that time, children were working up to 16 hours a day under terrible conditions in factories and cotton mills. In Great Britain, the Factory Act passed by Parliament in 1833 made it illegal for children under the age of nine to work in textile factories. Children between the ages of nine and 13 could work up to nine hours a day. Children 13 years and older could continue to work 12-hour days. Inspectors appointed to visit factories checked the birth certificates of the young workers, but factories managed to continue to illegally employ underage children.

To further protect workers, union organizations formed. They fought to defend the workers against abuse using the power of the strike. Before the unions organized, factory workers staged large walkouts to protest long working hours, insufficient wages, or unnecessarily dangerous working conditions.

In the early nineteenth century, unions formed at an amazing rate. By 1836, groups had formed unions in 13 American cities. All of these unions together formed the National Trades' Union. Not only did the unions fight for fair wages, better working conditions, and decent working hours, they also appointed people to enter the political arena to get laws passed to protect workers. The first union to attempt this was in Philadelphia. The union was driven to action because "living conditions in the Philadelphia slums were almost incredibly bad. Resentment against the increasing contrasts of urban wealth and poverty, excessively long hours of labor, low wages, lack of provision for free public education, imprisonment for small debts—these . . . brought about . . . the first labor party in America." [45]

WORKING CONDITIONS IN MINES

Thanks to the steam engine, the mining industry boomed. Workers of both sexes and all ages were employed, but the most unfortunate were the children. Some children began working as young as five years old. Most of these children died before they were 25.

Miners began to go deeper and deeper underground to mine precious coal and other minerals in 1834. A cage was used to safely transport them. Any able-bodied person could work in the dangerous, filthy mines. Men, women, and children flocked to them. Later, in the 1840s, the British Royal Commission reviewed the working conditions in mines. They created a report called the 1842 Mines and Collieries Act, which resulted in the banning of all women and girls and all boys under the age of 10 from working underground.

Many accidents and deaths occurred in the mines. Some mine owners may have tried to cover up these horrible incidents. In order to keep track of them, an 1850 act of Parliament required all mine owners to report fatal accidents to the Secretary of State.

Ten years later, in 1860, another act of Parliament raised the

Danger in the Mines

Mines were very dangerous places to work, both above and below the ground. Transporting workers from the surface to the mines was very risky. Large metal buckets carried men called sinkers, one leg in and one out, into the deep pits.

Danger was especially present for the young and the elderly. Many accidents claimed lives among these two groups. One explosion killed three children of ages ten, nine, and seven. A horse crushed one 11-year-old, and a metal cage crushed another. The wheels of a wagon trampled a 12-year-old and a 14-year-old. A 15-year-old engine boy became wrapped around the winder of an engine. A 13-year-old was killed when he fell down the shaft of a pumping machine.

Elderly workers also had many accidents that led to their deaths. A 72-year-old and a 75-year-old were killed in an explosion. A tub crushed a 76-year-old and a 70-year-old man. A 78-year-old laborer was run over by a locomotive. A falling stone ended the life of an 84-year-old man. The list goes on and on.

Even if death was not the final outcome, the long hours, repetitive movements, and hard physical labor took their toll on children. Their bodies became crippled or deformed from accidents or overuse. Sometimes their growth was stunted. The air at some factories was filled with poisonous gases. Children who could no longer work because of injuries had no future, because they had not been taught to read or write.

The mining industry profited immensely from the invention of the steam engine. Originally harnessed to pump standing water from underground mines, steam was also utilized to power the shovels used in strip mining. The advancements of steam engines in mining meant that even children could do the work, creating issues about child labor laws.

age minimum for miners, set specific requirements for the safe operation of underground transportation systems, and required areas known to be dangerous to be fenced off.

Even with all these precautions, accidents still happened. On January 16, 1862, a 21-ton beam snapped off and fell down the mineshaft. As it tumbled to the bottom, it broke off huge chunks of the shaft lining, trapping 204 miners. Herculean efforts were made to save the miners, but unfortunately they failed. All 204 men died because the shaft was the only way out of the mine. In response to this tragedy, Parliament again acted and required all mines to have two shafts.

Since the nineteenth century, job conditions have changed dramatically for the better as man relies more and more on machine power.

8 The Steam Engine Today

AT ISSUE

Even though the steam engine started the Industrial Revolution, it was not until the twentieth century that man began to form a heavy dependence on machine power. In the nineteenth century, animals performed more than half of all work, and wind and water were still used as power sources.

Only 100 years later, these statistics have changed markedly. In the year 2000, machines did about 98 percent of all work, with people and animals doing the remaining two percent. Dependence on machines is at an all-time high.

By the early twentieth century, the steam-powered engines were quickly being replaced by internal-combustion gasoline-driven engines. The heyday of steam was reaching its end. However, the discoveries of the steam-engine age are still in use today. Pistons and cylinders are integral to the engines of today's cars, motorcycles, tractors, and trucks.

In Europe, the railway continues to be a mainstay of land travel, although today all European trains are powered by electricity or diesel, not steam. Unfortunately, the train has slowly been losing its prominence in the United States. Airplanes have become the number-one choice of Americans.

Steam power, the driving force behind the Industrial Revolution in the nineteenth century, lost importance at the beginning of the twentieth century. However, steam engines are still used today.

This steam locomotive, built in 1912, pulls cars filled with sugar cane along the Arroyo Blanco line in Cuba. Other countries, such as China, Zimbabwe, and Russia, also still run steam locomotives for pleasure or transportation.

STEAM LOCOMOTIVES STILL IN USE

Some countries still use steam locomotives. China, which has steam trains that go to almost every city, still builds steam locomotives for hauling passengers and coal between towns.

In Zimbabwe, you can take a steam train for 360 miles (600 kilometers) from the capital, Harare, to the country's famed Victoria Falls. Kenya still runs a regular steam train service for 240 miles (400 kilometers) from its capital, Nairobi, to Mombasa on the Indian Ocean. Cuba still has steam locomotives that are used on sugar plantations.

Some countries, such as the United States, have steam locomotives running just for the sheer pleasure of them. A steam train runs regularly from Williams, Arizona, to the South Rim of the Grand Canyon. Also, in Russia, steam trains carry tourists to see the sights. Seeing a white cloud of smoke pouring from the chimney as the train clatters across the tracks brings back a bygone era.

MODERN STEAM POWER

Power plants as well as ships use steam turbines. A turbine is an engine that rotates by the pressure of steam, water, or air. These different forms of pressure hit vanes attached to a wheel that rotates on a rod or shaft.

Power plants powered by heat are called thermal power plants. These plants burn fuel such as wood, coal, oil, or natural gas to boil water in huge boilers. The steam is then piped to the turbine via thick-walled pipes. The steam moves the

Poisonous Pollutants

Along with a machine-driven society came pollution. Huge amounts of poisonous gases are emitted into the air daily by machines, and the cars driven by millions of people around the world are a major contributor. Also, factories and other industries are pumping poison into the air. Ways to curb these emissions are frantically being sought.

Prior to the invention of the steam engine, pollution was limited to garbage dumps and smoke from wood fires. Humankind at that time did not have to confront the massive pollution problems we face today.

The poisons in pollutants are linked to diseases such as cancer, leukemia, and multiple sclerosis. In the environment, pollutants have created acid rain, global warming, smog, and poisonous water that is killing massive ocean reefs. Animal species are threatened with or have already been driven to extinction due to pollutants. Many organizations have been formed to combat pollution and study its effect on the human body and the natural world.

Government regulations have been established to curb emissions from factories, mills, and vehicles.

Machines may have made our lives easier, but they have also created a much deadlier environment for us to live in.

turbine in a fast rotating motion, which turns the generator to produce electricity.

Nuclear power plants also use the power of steam. The only difference is that nuclear fission, which splits the nuclei of atoms, produces the heat to boil water and create steam. The steam is used to drive the turbines, which then turn the generators to produce electricity.

Steam turbines are also used on cruise ships, warships, and cargo ships. These turbines are a dependable source of power but are only part of the ship's engine.

Steam is also still used in Copenhagen, Denmark, and Russia as heat. A centralized boiler in each town pumps steam through thick pipes into each house. One major difference

Although steam engines and their mechanical and technological successors have made our lives easier by performing much of our work for us, these advancements haven't come without a price. The pollutants in the air, water, and soil of the world today are largely the result of the willingness to let machines do the things human muscles used to accomplish.

It is steam, not smoke, that drifts from the cooling towers of nuclear power plants. The energy produced by nuclear fission makes the steam that drives the turbines to generate electricity.

between the steam power of today and that of the last century is that today steam power is carefully monitored by computers, eliminating errors in steam pressure and water levels.

People continue to be fascinated by steam power. Museums display old steam engines and collectors buy and restore them with care. Steam fairs bring droves of people to see steam-powered tractors, compressors, pumps, and cars. Even though the steam engine is no longer the most commonly used source of power, it will always be remembered as the invention that kicked off the Industrial Revolution. We can thank its early inventors and the power of steam for the lifestyle of speed and convenience that we enjoy today.

A.D. 50–60 Hero creates the aeolipile.

1654 Otto von Guericke invents the first air pump.

1690 Denis Papin develops a cylinder with a piston driven by steam.

1712 Thomas Newcomen installs his atmospheric steam engine at a coal mine in Staffordshire.

1763 James Watt works on Newcomen steam engine and improves on the design.

1769 Watt obtains his first patent for improvements to his steam engine.

1769 Nicolas Cugnot's steam carriage travels at two to three miles per hour.

1773 Watt and Matthew Boulton form their business partnership.

1776 Watt's new engines are designed.

1782 Watt patents the double-acting engine.

1787 John Fitch displays to the public his boat driven by the power of steam.

1790 Watt creates the steam engine indicator.

1801 Patrick Miller, with the help of William Symington, develops steamboats.

1807 Robert Fulton sails successfully from New York City to Albany, New York in his steamboat, the *Clermont*.

1808 Richard Trevithick constructs a locomotive called *Catch-me-who-can* that he runs on a circular track for curious passengers.

1819 The steamship *Savannah* departs for England from Savannah, Georgia on May 22.

1827 Baltimore and Ohio Railroad Company is established.

1829 John Ericsson and John Braithwaite develop the first steam-pump fire engine.

1829 A New York engineer, Horatio Allen, imports the first full-size locomotive from England.

1830 On September 13, Robert Stephenson and Company makes a locomotive for the "Grand British Experimental Railway," the Liverpool & Manchester line. British royalty are the first passengers. The train runs at 15 to 25 miles per hour.

1860 The United States has 30,626 miles of laid railroad track. On June 16, the largest trans-Atlantic steamship, the *Great Eastern*, attempts its maiden voyage a second time and departs from Southampton, England, en route to New York City.

1867 S.H. Roper in the United States invents the first steam-powered bicycle.

1869 The Central Pacific and Union Pacific lines meet at Promontory Summit, Utah.

1870 Famous race between the steamboats *Natchez* and *Robert E. Lee.*

1890 A French inventor, Clement Ader, makes the first flight powered by steam.

1897 The Stanley brothers make their first steam-powered automobile.

1900 Steam-powered engines gradually begin to be replaced by internal-combustion gasoline-powered engines.

1934 George and William Besler publicly test the first working steam-engine airplane.

NOTES

Chapter 1

1. Mark Twain, *Roughing It.* New York: Harper & Row, 1871, p.20.
2. J.D. Storer, *A Simple History of the Steam Engine.* London: John Baker Publisher, 1969, p. 50.

Chapter 2

3. Quoted in Asa Briggs, *The Power of Steam.* Chicago: The University of Chicago Press, 1982, p. 17.
4. Briggs, *The Power of Steam*, p. 18.
5. Quoted in Briggs, *The Power of Steam*, p. 22.
6. Storer, *A Simple History of the Steam Engine*, p.35.
7. Richard L. Hills, *Power from Steam.* Cambridge, U.K.: Cambridge University Press, 1989, p. 89.
8. Quoted in Hills, *Power from Steam*, p. 31.
9. Quoted in Briggs, *The Power of Steam*, p. 32.

Chapter 3

10. Storer, *A Simple History of the Steam Engine*, p. 52.
11. Hills, *Power from Steam*, p. 55.
12. Quoted in Storer, *A Simple History of the Steam Engine*, p. 57.
13. Hills, *Power from Steam*, p. 66.
14. Briggs, *The Power of Steam*, p.57.
15. Hills, *Power from Steam*, p. 69.
16. Briggs, *The Power of Steam*, p. 58.

Chapter 4

17. Mark Twain, *Life on the Mississippi.* Pleasantville, N.Y.: The Reader's Digest Association, 1987, p. 37-38.
18. Quoted in Melvin Maddocks, *The Great Liners.* Alexandria, V.A.: Time-Life Books, 1978, p. 44.
19. Quoted in Ludovic Kennedy, *A Book of Sea Journeys.* New York: Rawson, Wade Publishers, Inc., 1981, p. 273.
20. Quoted in Maddocks, *The Great Liners*, p. 52-54.
21. Maddocks, *The Great Liners*, p. 60.
22. Quoted in Maddocks, *The Great Liners*, p. 58.
23. Maddocks, *The Great Liners*, p. 58.
24. Ibid., p. 60.
25. Robert O. Maguglin, *The Queen Mary: The Official Pictorial History.* Long Beach, C.A.: Albion Publishing Group, 1993, p. 48.

Chapter 5

26. Storer, *A Simple History of the Steam Engine*, p. 87.
27. Quoted in John Ackerman, *Yankees Under Steam.* Dublin, New Hampshire: Yankee, Inc., 1970, p. 25.
28. Ibid., p. 26.
29. Ibid., p. 37.
30. Ackerman, *Yankees Under Steam*, p. 205.

Chapter 6

31. Storer, *A Simple History of Steam Engine*, p. 95.
32. John Westwood, *The Colorful World of Steam.* London: Octopus Books Ltd., 1980, p. 8.
33. Ibid.
34. George H. Douglas, *All Aboard! The Railroad American Life.* New York: Paragon House, 1992, p. 43.
35. Charlton Ogburn, *Railroads: The Great American Adventure.* Washington, D.C.: National Georgaphic Society, 1977, p. 95.
36. Douglas, *All Aboard! The Railroad in American Life*, p. 188.
37. Jim Murphy, *Across America on an Emigrant Train*, New York: Clarion Books, 1993, p. 60
38. Ibid., p. 40.
39. Quoted in Ogburn, *Railroads: The Great American Adventure*, p. 134.

Chapter 7

40. Quoted in George Rogers Taylor, *The Transportation Revolution: 1815-1860.* New York: Harper & Row, 1951, p. 132.
41. Taylor, *The Transportation Revolution: 1815-1860*, p. 63.
42. Ibid., p. 74.
43. Ibid., p. 227-228.
44. Quoted in John Westwood, *Railways at War.* San Diego: Howell-North Books, 1980, p. 186.
45. Taylor, *The Transportation Revolution: 1815-1860*, p. 258.

Ackerman, John. *Yankees Under Steam.* Dublin, N.H.: Yankee, Inc., 1970.

Briggs, Asa. *The Power of Steam.* Chicago: The University of Chicago Press, 1982.

Douglas, George H. *All Aboard! The Railroad in American Lives.* St. Paul, Minn.: Paragon House, 1992.

Ellis, C. Hamilton. *Railways.* New York: Peebles Press, 1974.

Hills, Richard L. *Power From Steam* Cambridge, U.K.: Cambridge University Press, 1989.

Kennedy, Ludovic. *A Book of Sea Journeys.* New York: Rawson, Wade Publishers, Inc., 1981.

Maddocks, Melvin. *The Great Liners,* by Alexandria, Va.: Time-Life Books Inc., 1978. Maguglin, Robert O. *The Queen Mary.* Long Beach, C.A.: Albion Publishing Group, 1993.

Murphy, Jim. *Across America on an Emigrant Train.* New York: Clarion Books, 1993.

Neider, Charles, ed. *The Complete Humorous Sketches and Tales of Mark Twain.* New York: Doubleday and Company, 1961.

Siegel, Beatrice. *The Steam Engine.* New York: Walker and Company, 1986.

Storer, J. D. *A Simple History of the Steam Engine.* London: John Baker Publisher, 1969.

Taylor, George Rogers. *The Transportation Revolution: 1815–1860.* New York: Harper and Row, 1968.

Twain, Mark. *Life on the Mississippi.* Pleasantville, N.Y.: The Reader's Digest Association, Inc., 1987.

———. *Roughing It.* New York: Harper and Row, 1817.

Westwood, John. *Railways at War.* San Diego: Howell-North Books, 1980.

———. *The Colorful World of Steam.* London: Octopus Books, Ltd., 1980.

Briggs, Asa. *The Power of Steam.* Chicago: The University of Chicago Press, 1982.

Ellis, C. Hamilton. *Railways.* New York: Peebles Press, 1974.

Hills, Richard L. *Power From Steam.* Cambridge, U.K.: Cambridge University Press, 1989.

Ogburn, Charlton. *Railroads: The Great American Adventure.* Washington, D.C.: National Geographic Society, 1977.

Siegel, Beatrice. *The Steam Engine.* New York: Walker and Company, 1986.

Storer, J.D. *A Simple History of the Steam Engine.* London: John Baker Publisher, 1969.

Taylor, George Rogers. *The Transportation Revolution: 1815–1860.* New York: Harper and Row, 1968

Westwood, John. *Railways at War.* Oxford, U.K.: Osprey Publishing Limited, 1980.

WEBSITES

Brunel—The *Great Eastern*
http://sol.brunel.ac.uk/~jarvis/brunelstory/greateastern.html

How Stuff Works: How Steam Engines Work
http://travel.howstuffworks.com/steam.htm

Richard Trevithick 1803 Steam Carriage
http://www.brooklands.org.uk/Goodwood/g9828.htm

RMS *Queen Mary*, Long Beach
http://www.queenmary.com/

Stanley Steamers, White and Doble Steam Cars
http://www.stanleysteamers.com/

Steam Engine Library
http://www.history.rochester.edu/steam/

World of Steam
http://www.worldofsteam.com/

page:

7: © Tom Bean/CORBIS
9: © Gianni Dagli Orti/CORBIS
14: © Bettmann/CORBIS
17: Science Museum/Science & Society Picture Library
20: © Hulton/Archive by Getty Images, Inc.
23: © Tom McCloskey
27: © Bettmann/CORBIS
30: © Tom McCloskey
34: © Michael Nicholson/CORBIS
37: © Bettmann/CORBIS
39: © Archivo Iconografico, S.A./ CORBIS
42: © Hulton/Archive by Getty Images, Inc.
46: © Hulton/Archive by Getty Images, Inc.
49: © Bettmann/CORBIS
52: Courtesy of the Smithsonian Institution, NMAH/Transportation

54: © CORBIS
57: © Bettmann/CORBIS
58: Courtesy of Joe Kras
61: © Bettmann/CORBIS
64: © Underwood & Underwood/ CORBIS
67: © Sean Sexton Collection/CORBIS
68: © CORBIS
71: © Bettmann/CORBIS
76: © Minnesota Historical Society/COR-BIS
79: © CORBIS
83: © CORBIS
85: © Colin Garratt; Milepost 92 1/2/ CORBIS
87: Eyewire Getty Images
88: © Royalty-Free/CORBIS

Cover: © Bettmann/CORBIS
Frontis: © Hulton/Archive by Getty Images, Inc.

ABOUT THE AUTHOR

Sara Louise Kras has had several nonfiction books published in the educational field, including the Chelsea House book *Anwar Sadat* in the MAJOR WORLD LEADERS series. She has worked in education for 15 years and has traveled extensively throughout the world. After completing an educational project in Zimbabwe, Africa, she now lives in Glendale, California.

ACKNOWLEDGEMENTS

I would like to thank Scott and Carol Higgins for getting us into the steam show at Vista, California, and answering all my many questions on steam engines.

I would also like to thank my cousin, John Van Amburg, for answering all my questions on steam locomotives and sharing his love of steam engines with me.

I would like to thank Captain Ron Bell and Dirk Drossel of the Burbank Fire Department for giving us a personalized tour of the fire department museum and allowing us to take photos of the rebuilt Burbank steam fire engine.